Archives & Manuscripts:
An Introduction to Automated Access

H. Thomas Hickerson

BASIC MANUAL SERIES

Society of American Archivists   Chicago, 1981

Third Printing

© 1981   The Society of American Archivists, 600 S. Federal, Suite 504, Chicago, Illinois 60605. All Rights Reserved.

ISBN# 931828-29-5

Library of Congress Catalog #81-52113

Foreword

Each year the Society of American Archivists significantly expands the list of publications available to the archival profession. The five-volume Basic Manual Series which was published in 1977 offers archivists information on the basic archival functions. This series includes manuals on *Appraisal and Accessioning, Arrangement and Description, Reference and Access, Security,* and *Surveys.*

The second series, of which this manual is a part, addresses some of the specialized interests and concerns of archivists and manuscript curators. This series will include manuals on *Automated Access, Cartographic Records and Architectural Drawings, Exhibits, Museum Archives, Public Programs,* and *Reprography.*

The Society is most grateful to the National Historical Publications and Records Commission, whose support has made possible the publication of this manual series.

Ruth W. Helmuth, *President*
Society of American Archivists

Contents

Preface

That the implementation of automated techniques for access to archives and manuscripts has been chosen as a topic in the Society of American Archivists' Basic Manual Series affirms my belief that computers are a basic tool for archivists, and that an introduction to computer use for intellectual access to and control of archives and manuscripts should be available. This does not mean that I support their use in all processes in all repositories, and I hope that the reader will find that I have consistently adopted a critical approach in my examination of the use of computers by archivists. I do believe, however, that for some common archival processes, computers can provide accurate and efficient assistance, and that archival automation is opening a new realm of possibilities for the management and use of historical documentation.

My efforts to provide an effective introduction to automated access will be, at best, only a modest success. Some difficulties are obvious; the manual can be neither comprehensive nor truly current. So much research is being conducted in the information sciences, it is impossible for an individual to be aware of all findings pertinent to archival operations. This situation is complicated by the remarkable speed of technological growth throughout society. But of far greater significance to the writing of this manual is the experimental stage that archival automation is in currently.

The application of electronic data processing (EDP) for the management of archives and manuscripts has been seriously considered for only about fifteen years, and, only during the last five years, has there been an appreciable increase in the number and variety of applications. While we can draw on the work of many disciplines, particularly those engaged in by our colleagues in libraries, museums and records management programs, archives are unique, and we have to develop approaches specifically suited to archival needs. Belonging to a small, tradition-oriented profession faced with many new challenges, archivists are only now generating the initiative and support necessary to develop these approaches.

Current trends suggest that during the next five years the growth in the use of EDP use by archivists may be rapid; a complete "how to" manual could be very useful. Unfortunately, while a detailed instructional handbook is needed now, we have yet to develop a corpus of shared experience or critical literature on which to draw.

In the course of preparing this manual, I have traveled and consulted extensively and have uniformly received generous and beneficial cooperation from archivists and librarians, but we have yet to establish proven formulas, and each application I investigated was, essentially, an innovation. Furthermore, as a profession, we are only beginning to develop the national policies, research support, and communication and mutual-support networks needed to facilitate the implementation of automated techniques or to analyze the future implications of current developments. Consequently, with the forebearance of the editors, this manual is a combination of introductory handbook, descriptive review and critical essay.

Introduction

Establishing effective intellectual control over the historical records currently housed in American archival repositories is a formidable task. During the twentieth century, growth in the rate of production of recorded information has been astounding. This growth has led to a substantial increase in the number of archival repositories and a rapid expansion of the archival profession, although the increase in the number of archivists is in no way equivalent to the expansion in the size of our holdings. Archivists have had to develop new techniques to deal with the billions of documents under their control.

At the same time that they are faced with the complexities of the information explosion, archivists are also witnessing an expansion in the number and variety of uses of archival holdings. Practitioners of the "new social history," social scientists, and genealogists have contributed to a change in the number and nature of user requests. Traditional finding aids have often proven inadequate in meeting their needs. These researchers seek to step across traditional boundaries of archival organization, needing common access points for different types of historical documentation within a single repository or in several repositories.

Both the increased volume of archival holdings and the expansion of their use suggest that innovative application of EDP could benefit archivists considerably. Indeed, while early uses of automation in archival repositories were primarily for item indexing of traditional sources, in the last five years, the trend has changed. Archival use of automation is expanding, and archivists are now developing repository-wide or even nation-wide applications of EDP. This manual is designed to facilitate this growth of archival automation.

Chapter I, "Computers and How They Work," provides an introduction to the basic concepts of computer operation and acquaints the reader with terminology used in describing these operations. The second chapter, "Computer Operation and Archival Objectives," continues the introductory examination of computer activities, focusing on aspects of computer operation which have particular relevance for archivists. Chapter III surveys "Archivists and Computers at Work." This examination of several computer systems and their use by archivists is intended to convey a sense of what is being done and to illustrate some basic questions concerning archival automation. Chapter IV, "Implementing Automated Techniques," examines steps in the design and development of automated processes for institutional application and reviews efforts and opportunities for national cooperation. Each chapter is followed by a brief list of Suggested Readings.* This manual seeks to stimulate the development of effective policies and practices for the use of computers by the archival profession.

---

*A comprehensive bibliography, *Automation, Machine-Readable Records, and Archival Administration: An Annotated Bibliography,* has been compiled and edited by Richard M. Kesner and published by the Society of American Archivists (1980).

1 Computers and How They Work

The splitting of the atom and the exploration of space have been more spectacular; automobiles and television are more visible; but the invention of the electronic *digital computer** will also have to be considered a major factor in shaping the nature of human society in the second half of the twentieth century. Influential in many areas of modern life, computers are of particular importance to information managers. No other development since the invention of movable type has had as great an effect on the production, dissemination, storage, and use of information as has that of the electronic computer, and this development has only been in process for about thirty-five years. Compared to the other great inventions in information communication (writing, begun about 5,000 years ago; the alphabet, developed some 3,000 years ago; movable type, invented about 700 years ago), the computer is only in its infancy.[1]

Archivists will document the role of computers in shaping modern society, and they will maintain computer-generated documentation concerning many aspects of twentieth-century life. Like other managers, they will use computer assistance to maintain administrative control of their holdings of textual, audiovisual, and *machine-readable* records. To serve their clients efficiently, they will use computers to provide intellectual access to the informational content of their holdings. Yet, as with many twentieth-century developments, computers will not suit every organization or resolve all archival problems; archivists should implement automated methods with caution, care, and wisdom.

One purpose of this manual is to facilitate the development of a critical approach to the use of computers by archivists. This chapter is intended to provide general knowledge concerning the basic concepts of computer operation and to acquaint the reader with terminology used in describing these operations. It is not necessary for an archivist to have a technical understanding of computers, nor to possess programming skills, in order to implement an automated information retrieval system successfully.[2] If you wish to use an automobile to get to your job each morning, it is much more important that you know where you are going than that you understand the operating principles of internal combustion engines. Effective automobile use requires a sense of the capabilities and limitations of your automobile, familiarity with those parts of the automobile that interface directly with the vehicle user, and an awareness of the basic protocols for vehicle operation in your immediate environment. Archivists need similar types of knowledge concerning computers.

An *electronic digital computer* is an information processing machine which can perform substantial computation, including numerous arithmetic or logic operations, without intervention by a human operator during the process. The term electronic indicates that the computer is powered by electrical and electronic devices. Digital refers to discrete symbols, including letters of the alphabet, numbers, and algebraic and business symbols.[3] The computer accepts the information (*data*), performs operations on it, and provides the results of those operations. This processing of data takes place with considerable speed, accuracy, and reliability.[4]

The central units of computers are largely constructed of thousands of millions of high-speed, on/off switches organized so that sets of processing instructions (*programs*) and the data to be processed can be recorded and stored in the computer. These switches respond to electrical signals. By using a code, these signals can represent numbers and letters. Most modern computers use a code based on the *binary number system*, which uses only two symbols. Each symbol is called a *bit* (the smallest unit of information in a binary system), and each bit may be either a one or a zero. "1" can mean "yes," "on," or the quantity "one"; "0" can mean "no," "off," or the quantity "none." By using these two symbols, any number or letter can be represented.

The following list shows how the decimals from 0 to 10 can be represented by using a four-bit *binary code:*

Decimal	Binary
0	0000
1	0001
2	0010
3	0011
4	0100
5	0101
6	0110
7	0111
8	1000
9	1001
10	1010

---

*Italicized terms are defined in the Glossary.

[1] Joe B. Wyatt, "Technology and the Library," *College and Research Libraries* 40 (March 1979): 121.

[2] David Bearman, "Automated Access to Archival Information: Assessing Systems," *American Archivist* 42,181.

[3] *Analog computers* process data represented in a continuous form, usually represented by physical variables, such as voltage, resistance, or rotation. They are not used in the type of *language processing* discussed in this manual.

[4] Richard C. Dorf, *Computers and Man*, 27-31.

The following list shows how the letters of the alphabet can be represented by using a six-bit binary code:

A = 11001	N = 100101
B = 110010	O = 100110
C = 110011	P = 100111
D = 110100	Q = 101000
E = 110101	R = 101001
F = 110110	S = 010010
G = 110111	T = 010011
H = 111000	U = 010100
I = 111001	V = 010101
J = 100001	W = 010110
K = 100010	X = 010111
L = 100011	Y = 011000
M = 100100	Z = 011001

The user enters alphabetic data which the computer stores and processes in binary form.

W	0 1 0 1 1 0
O	1 0 0 1 1 0
O	1 0 0 1 1 0
D	1 1 0 1 0 0
Y	0 1 1 0 0 0
G	1 1 0 1 1 1
U	0 1 0 1 0 0
T	0 1 0 0 1 1
H	1 1 1 0 0 0
R	1 0 1 0 0 1
I	1 1 1 0 0 1
E	1 1 0 1 0 1

In operating most large computers, an eight-bit binary code is used. An eight-position binary unit is called a *byte*. A byte can represent 256 different things, including uppercase or lowercase letters, numbers, punctuation marks, special symbols, or specific commands to the computer. This binary system, invented by an English mathematician, George Boole (1815-1864), and adapted for computer use in the mid-1940s by John Von Neumann, is an essential element in modern computer operations.

While the binary system provides computers with a means of expression, the processing of data is carried out by a group of interconnected components combined into what is called a *hardware* system (physical equipment).[5] The major hardware components are a *central processing unit* (*CPU*), *main memory,* and *input and output* (*I/O*) devices.

The CPU is the active part of the computer, either doing the work we want done or directing what is done. It has two primary components, the *control unit* and the *arithmetic-logic unit.* The control unit acts as the executive of the computer, directing what is to be done next and calling other units into operation when appropriate. The arithmetic-logic unit adds, subtracts, multiplies, and divides numbers and performs comparisons on nonnumeric data. The CPU also includes registers which hold data temporarily and a *register* or register-like device which keeps track of what is going on at any given time.[6]

---

[5] The term *system* is used frequently in this manual. Although most often used in reference to an integrated set of computer programs, it is also used in reference to computer equipment, archival programs, or other assemblies of methods, procedures, techniques, machinery, or personnel united by regulated interaction to form a whole or to accomplish a set of specific functions.

[6] James Joyce, "Hardware for the Humanist: What You Should Know and Why," *Computers and the Humanities* 11, 301-302.

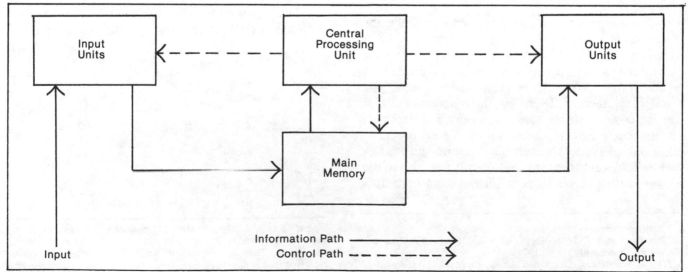

Figure 1. Simplified block diagram of a computer system

Main memory is a *storage* device for both the information to be processed and the instructions for processing. It accepts data from input devices, exchanges data with and supplies instructions to the CPU and conveys data to output units. All information to be processed must pass through main memory; therefore, the unit must be able to retain an adequate amount of data and the necessary processing instructions.[7] In addition to storage capacity, computer effectiveness is also determined by the *access time* of a memory unit (the interval of time required to locate and transfer data to and from storage). The faster the arithmetic speed of a computer, the larger and faster the main memory must be.[8]

Data to be processed must be conveyed to the machine in machine-readable form. The computer communicates the results of processing in a visually readable form, in a machine-readable form, or in both. If machine-readable, these results may be used as entry data for additional processing or stored for future use. Information and processing instructions are transferred to main memory and the results are recorded by input/output equipment. These devices are called *peripheral equipment* because they provide the system with outside communication, enabling us to direct the operation of the computer, and because they are often physically located a considerable distance from the CPU and memory unit. The best known input form is the *punched card,* and the best known output form is the *printout.*

While keypunch machines are still in use, the variety of data entry equipment is steadily growing. Most of the newer devices are variations of *key-to-tape* inscribers, *on-line* terminals, or *intelligent terminals* (terminals which have a small computer enclosed within the terminal case).

Key-to-tape inscribers, such as IBM's Magnetic Tape/Selectric Typewriter (MT/ST) encode data on magnetic tape cassettes. MT/ST cassettes can be used to produce typescript documents, allowing additions, deletions, and changes of text without requiring major retyping. The same tape cassette can be used as computer input if it is run through a machine which converts the data on the cassette to a magnetic tape of the proper size and density to be used as computer input.[9] Most key-to-tape inscribers, often referred to as *word processing* devices, operate in a manner similar to the MT/ST. Some can be equipped with a *cathode ray tube* (*CRT*) where the text can be displayed as it is typed. Others, such as IBM's Magnetic Card/Selectric Typewriter (MC/ST), can be operated as an on-line terminal (the I/O device is connected to a central computer). The MC/ST records data on a 3½-by-8-inch magnetic card. These data may be transmitted by telephone lines directly to the computer.[10]

---

[7]Storage capacity is commonly measured in K's, a K being the equivalent of 1000 bytes (characters).

[8]Dorf, *Computers and Man,* 112-115.

[9]Computer tapes have seven or nine tracks, and usually the data is stored on them at a density of either 800 or 1600 *bits per inch (bpi)*.

[10]Robert G. Chenhall, *Museum Cataloging in the Computer Age,* 85-86.

Figure 2. An IBM Card Data Recorder. (Photograph by Deborah Gesensway)

Computer *terminals* consist of a keyboard quite similar to that of an electric typewriter, circuitry for translating a depressed key into a computer code for the desired character, and a CRT for displaying characters. The terminal may be connected to the computer by a direct wire *(hardwired)* or through a telephone data set which is connected to a telephone company line. Terminals may be permanently wired into telephone circuits, or portable terminals can be connected through an ordinary telephone headset with the use of an acoustic coupler. Once the terminal is connected to a central computer, the terminal operator can enter data directly to the computer and has access to many of the editing, processing, and storage capabilities of the computer. After the operator has recorded the data in the desired format, the computer can be instructed to process the data immediately, or the data may be recorded on *magnetic tape* or *magnetic disk* (a mass-storage device which can hold many files of data, stored in circular tracks, each with a unique location) for future processing.

Figure 3. CPT 4200 word processing typewriter. (Photograph courtesy of the Washington State Historical Records Advisory Board)

Intelligent terminals (also called smart terminals) have built-in *minicomputers* or *microcomputers* and have considerable independent capability for editing data and general processing. Results may be displayed on a CRT or a *line printer* may be attached for producing *hard copy* (a printed copy of computer output in a visually readable form). Some smart terminals store data on a cassette tape or on a *floppy disk* (a small magnetic disk, usually consisting of a single recording surface, also called a *diskette*). These terminals can be operated as independent self-contained computers or may be used to communicate with larger computers when the size of the data base or the processing re-

Figure 4. A Datamedia 1521 being used for *on-line data entry*. (Photograph by Deborah Gesensway)

quirements so demand.[11]

Although key-to-tape and *key-to-disk* systems are the primary alternatives to punched card use, *punched paper tape, magnetic ink character recognition* (*MICR*), and *optical character recognition* (*OCR*) are also used for data entry in some special applications.

Computer output, in addition to the familiar printout, may be displayed on a CRT, or may be printed in newspaper, magazine, or book format through the use of *electronic photocomposition. Computer output microfilm* (*COM*) is increasingly common. A COM printer converts data directly from magnetic tape to microfiche or roll film. COM production is cheaper and faster than printout production, and the film occupies much less space. Film duplicates are inexpensive to produce and to distribute, and microfilm has much better retention characteristics than the standard printout paper.[12] The variety of output forms continues to expand. In the near future, access to an information retrieval system, which will display textual and graphic information on residential television sets (Viewdata), will be offered to general users in the United States.[13]

This chapter provides only a modest introduction to computer operations. Archivists need more detailed knowledge of those aspects of automated systems that relate most directly to their effective implementation in archives.

[11] Daniel L. Slotnick and Joan K. Slotnick, *Computers: Their Structure, Use, and Influence* (Englewood Cliffs, N.J.: Prentice-Hall, Inc., 1979), 349.

[12] Joel A. Shirley, "Data Entry and Output at the South Carolina Archives," *SPINDEX Users Conference: Proceedings of a Meeting Held at Cornell University, Ithaca, New York, March 31 and April 1, 1978,* ed. H. Thomas Hickerson, 55-57.

[13] "Viewdata Service to be Developed in the U.S. by INSAC," *Information Retrieval & Library Automation* 15 (July 1979): 4.

Suggested Readings

Chenhall, Robert G. *Museum Cataloging in the Computer Age.* Nashville, Tenn.: American Association for State and Local History, 1975.

Davis, William S., and McCormack, Allison. *The Information Age.* Reading, Mass.: Addison-Wesley Publishing Company, 1979.

Dorf, Richard C. *Computers and Man.* 2nd ed. San Francisco: Boyd & Fraser Publishing Co., 1977.

Joyce, James. "Hardware for the Humanist: What You Should Know and Why." *Computers and the Humanities* 11 (September/October 1977): 299-307.

2   Computer Operation and Archival Objectives

The preceding chapter primarily concerned the major computer hardware components and the use of binary coding. This chapter begins with a description of methods for directing the functioning of computers and then focuses on the organization of data for computer processing. As our examination of computer activities continues, we will direct increasing attention to those aspects of computer operation which have particular relevance for archivists. Special consideration is given to the further development of familiarity with basic *electronic data processing* (*EDP*) terminology. For archivists this process is complicated by the fact that certain terms, which have special definitions in archival practice, also have special meanings in the application of EDP, e.g., file, record, and documentation. A significant portion of the chapter is devoted to defining special terms and explaining their significance for archivists. This chapter is intended to prepare archivists to identify and evaluate characteristics and capabilities of automated systems which are important to the fulfillment of their own particular needs.

Computer operation is directed by *software* (a collective term for programs). Software consists of series of instructions which tell a computer, step by step, what it is to do. Each instruction tells the computer to perform one of its basic functions. These functions are restricted to various forms of the following: (1) addition; (2) subtraction; (3) multiplication; (4) division; (5) copying; (6) yes/no logic (compare); (7) request input; (8) request output.

If these instructions are in the right sequence and correctly written, the computer will carry out the prescribed steps effectively, converting input data to accurate output information. It is both a comforting and frustrating feature of computers that they can do nothing unless humans provide them with very clear and concise instructions.[14]

There are two basic kinds of software. The kind most commonly referred to is *application software*, which contains the instructions of specific users. There is also *system software*, which is a set of programs that belongs to the entire system rather than to any single user and usually performs a support function. *Operating systems*, the primary type of system software, are special programs grouped together in a single region of the computer's memory which cannot be altered by the user. This kind of control software manages the internal coordination of the resources of the computer when numerous application programs request processing of data at the same time. This makes possible the *time-sharing* (the interleaved use of the time of a device) arrangements common to large computer centers which allow many users to obtain access almost simultaneously to a single central processing unit.[15]

System software is essential for the large-scale use of computers and makes possible the economical use of EDP. However, archivists are much more concerned with application software, and the following references to sets of programs or systems relate to application software.

Perhaps the first fact that archivists should understand about software systems (software packages) is that not all programs will run (operate) on all computers. While this may seem reasonable, the degree to which it is true may be surprising.

A frequent limit on compatibility is the language of the software. Computer programs are written in *programming or source languages*. Using these languages, instructions are translated by the computer system software into a machine-level binary code (object code) which the central processing unit can implement. There are numerous programming languages; the most widely used, *FORTRAN* (FORmula TRANslator) and *COBOL* (COmmon Business Oriented Language), can be used with many different types and brands of computers. Other *high-level languages* have been tailored to the needs of specific communities of users or designed for use with a specific brand of equipment. *Assembly-level languages*, which are manufacturer-designed for use with a certain brand and size of computer, equate closely to *machine-level language*. Although the programs in

---

[14]William S. Davis and Allison McCormack, *The Information Age*, 144-145.

[15]*Ibid.*, 184-193.

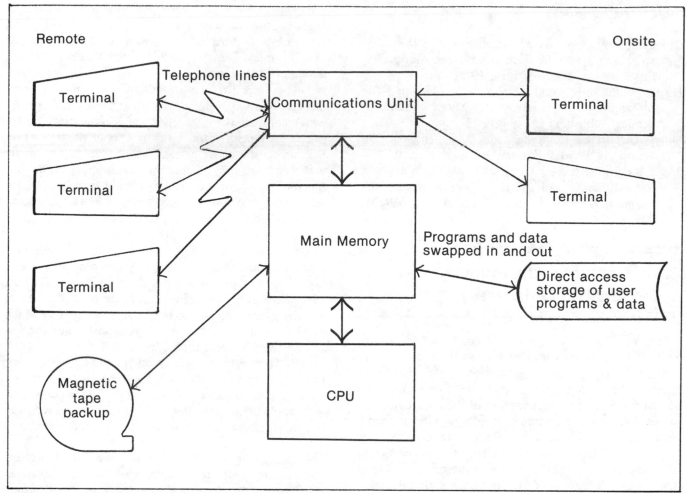

Figure 5.   A diagram of a time-sharing network

some systems are written in more than one language, most are not. Since a system may include many programs,[16] it requires considerable effort to rewrite a system in an additional language. Thus, the degree to which a system is transportable (the ease with which it can be used on different brands and models of computers) is influenced by the language in which it is programmed.

A set of programs is transmitted to the main memory of a computer in the same manner that other data is transmitted (e.g., cards, tape). Once stored in memory, the programs tell the computer how the data is organized, how to recognize it, and what to do with it. Archivists have to organize the data to be processed into

a structured series of information called a *file* (a collection of related computer records which, because they are similar, can be organized and processed as a unit). The manner in which such files (collectively referred to as a *data base*), are created, organized, and maintained is a significant characteristic of any computerized system.[17]

A file is comprised of *records* (collections of related, similarly structured items of data, each treated as a unit). At an archival repository, in a file containing folder-level indexing data for an administrative correspondence series, all of the descriptive information concerning the contents of a particular folder (e.g., folder title, names of correspondents, and inclusive dates) would be recorded in a single record. Each of these pieces of information is recorded in a *field* or *data field* (a specified area used for recording particular

---

[16]One program does not a system make. The output from one program is usually the input for another; one program alphabetizes a group of terms; the next program prints them out. Most language-processing systems have at least three programs: one to input data, one to sort data, and one to output results. Most systems include many more, although not all the programs in a complex system will need to be used in every application.

[17]Special files can be created and dissolved in the process of building and maintaining a master file (the primary, current edition of a file), e.g., input files or update files.

The following is a list showing the tag structure used by the L.D.S. Church Historical Department in its basic finding aid. All the indexing tags have the function indicator 3 so they are field indexed as one term. The 100, 110, 400, 600, 900, 901, 902, 903, 904, and 905 tags are used for the Guide (ARSP5). The main index uses 110, 120, 200, and 210 tags as keywords with the 100, 110, 400, and 600 tags providing information under the keywords. The Special Lists index uses 700 and 730 tags for keywords with the 100, 110, and 710 tags appearing under the keywords.

Tag Number	Field Number	Description
000	Control Number	The control number is based on the collection number therefore MSD 1234 (which is a manuscript collection) has the control number A01234.
100	Title	The title includes the author or creator usually a generic title and span dates of the documents. An example is SMITH, JOSEPH, PAPERS, 1827-1844.
110	Significant Title	We use this tag only when a title needs to appear in the index.
120	Main Entry	This is the author or creator of the collection. Personal names are entered last name first. Birth and death dates are included when possible. An example is YOUNG, BRIGHAM, 1801-1877. The 120 tags never end with a period so that main entries and subject entries are separate in the index.
200	Supplied Subjects	This tag includes subjects from our authority list, place names, and buildings. (201-209 and 20A-20Z can also be used.)
210	Personal Name and Organization Subjects	Personal names can be entered as added entries (YOUNG, 1801-1877 - AUTHOR) or as subjects (YOUNG, BRIGHAM, 1807-1877). The names of Church auxiliaries and departments or corporate names would also be entered under this tag. Examples are DESERET SUNDAY SCHOOL UNION. and CANNON, GRANT AND COMPANY. (210-219 and 21A-21Z are used as needed.) The 210 tags always end in a period to separate them from a corresponding main entry.
400	Collection Number	The numbers are right justified so as to be more readable. Examples are MSDxxxxx72 and MSDxxx1234. (An x is used to indicate the number of spaces entered.)
600	Film Number	Many of the department's collections have been microfilmed. The film has a separate number. The fourth item on film 162 would be entered as Fxx162#x4. (An x is used to indicate the number of spaces used.)
700	Donor	Personal names of donors are entered last name first. If the originals are in private possession or at another institution then one space proceeds the entry. Example is xYALE UNIVERSITY LIBRARY. The 700, 710, and 730 tags are used to produce a separate index we call "Special Lists."
710	Date Donated	Only the year is entered
730	Special Lists	Special Lists are produced by entering two spaces followed by a two digit abbreviation. Examples are: Journals-- xxJR, Language--xxL:xxSPANISH, Restrictions--xxR:1995, Daguerreotypes-- xxDG.
900	Collation	Volume, size, form. Examples are: xx1V. 37CM. MS., and xx3FT. MS.
901	First Content Note	This provides the researcher with brief information about the creator and a description of what material and potentially useful information the collection contains.
902	Second Content Note	Used if the content note needs to be divided into two paragraphs.
903	Donor/Source Note	The donor is listed if we have the originals. An example is xxGIFT OF JAMES D. MOYLE, SALT LAKE CITY, UTAH, 1975.
904	Restriction Notes	Explains any restrictions to use of the collection. Examples are xxCLOSED UNTIL 1995 EXCEPT BY PERMISSION OF THE DONOR, xxCLOSED EXCEPT BY PERMISSION OF THE CHURCH ARCHIVIST.
905	Finding Aids Note	An example is: xxSEE REGISTER FOR COMPLETE LIST.

Figure 6. Tag structure and field use guidelines. Figure 6 shows the tag structure used by the Historical Department of the Church of Jesus Christ of Latter-day Saints to produce a guide to their holdings. (Reprinted, by permission, from Brent G. Thompson, "Guide Project Tag Structure," in SPINDEX Users Conference, ed. H. Thomas Hickerson, p. 117-119.)

categories or elements of data). In a donor file each record might contain a field for the donor's name and an additional field for the title of each manuscript collection given by that donor. In a folder-level index there could be separate fields for the folder title, inclusive dates, names of correspondents, and subject keywords. While a system may require that certain fields in a record be used for specific functions, the functions of most can be assigned by the user.

Assigning fields is one of the most important aspects of designing a computer application. Because the computer searches for field location, rather than content, fields must always appear either in the same physical space within a record (fixed location) or in the same relative position with their precise beginning identified by a specific *tag* (usually an alpha/numeric code, called a tag, *field-tag* or *data tag*). One must use consistent field assignments throughout a file. For example, within an accessions file the same field in each record must be used for the accession date or it might be very difficult to produce a chronological listing of accessions. If a multi-institutional data base (large accumulated files of information in machine-readable form for subsequent access by computer) is created, all participants must use similar field assignments and tag structures. Thus, a field should be well defined as to the category of information to be recorded in that field and the function or functions for which that information might be used.

Tag structures must be carefully designed. To do this, one must be familiar with archival methodology and have a clear understanding of what one expects a system to provide. One must also be familiar with characteristics of automated systems which determine how effective a particular system will be in meeting the needs of archivists.

An important system characteristic is record length; almost all systems have a specified maximum number of characters that can be included in each record. Though archivists are sometimes verbose, they do have a legitimate need for ample record capacities. A length of 5,000 to 10,000 characters is appropriate, and systems with maximum record lengths of 2,000 or less characters will probably be ineffective for a broad range of archival uses.[18] This excludes a surprisingly large

number of systems, including some designed for library use. Although reprogramming is possible, and length limitations may be circumvented by the use of associated records, this does not always provide the desired results.

Adequate field length is also important,[19] but perhaps even more significant than maximum record and field lengths is that those lengths be variable (the length may vary up to a set maximum). Some systems require that all records be of a specified length (*fixed-length*) and include a certain number of fields of specified length. Fixed-length records and fixed-length fields are common in business systems, but archivists will usually need systems with variable-length records, *variable-length fields*, and variable-occurrence fields (some fields may or may not be present in every record). Archival documents do not have uniform bibliographic data, and archivists do not wish to describe all segments of their holdings with the same degree of detail.

Another aspect of system structure is data base arrangement and *access*. Access methods significantly influence the use one can make of a data base. Even within some specific systems, different files can be accessed differently. While there are a variety of arrangement schemes, there are two basic types, those that provide *sequential access* and those that provide *direct access*.

In a sequential access file, the data is usually arranged serially, either numerically or alphabetically, and the file must be searched and processed serially. This method is designed to facilitate *batch processing* (a type of *off-line* processing in which computer operations are programmed ahead of time so that in executing the set of programs each is completed before the next program in the set begins). Typically, data, stored sequentially on magnetic tape, is run through a set of programs in a predetermined order, and the results are printed in a predesigned format. In an archival repository this method can be effective and cost-efficient for producing a variety of printed listings and indexes. Few sequential access systems are programmed to allow on-line searching and information display at an interactive terminal because on-line, serial searches of large files could be very slow and expensive.

A direct access system is capable of locating and using information at any location within a storage device in a constant amount of time. Every location available for data storage on a direct access device is

---

[18]In 1965, the Hoover Institution on War, Revolution and Peace applied an IBM 1401 Library Program which had a 320 character limit to the records of the American Relief Administration. That length was found to be inadequate, and the limit was expanded to 2,200. H. Thomas Hickerson, Joan Winters, and Venetia Beale, *SPINDEX II at Cornell and a Review of Archival Automation in the United States*, 18-20. The initial OS (operating system) version of SPINDEX II (Selective Permutation INDEXing) had a maximum character length of 1,981 characters. This was found to be inadequate for National Ar-

chives and Records Service users, and the maximum length was expanded to 7,000 characters. Stephen Hannestad, "The Role of the National Archives in the Future Development and Maintenance of SPINDEX," *SPINDEX Users Conference*, ed. H. Thomas Hickerson, 91-92.

[19]A length of 700 characters or more is desirable.

identified by its own unique, numeric address. Data stored on magnetic disks, the most common direct access storage device, is recorded on the magnetic surface of a flat circular plate in a series of concentric circles called *tracks*. Individual bits are denoted by magnetized spots; bits are organized to form *characters*; characters are grouped to form fields; and so on.

A magnetic disk is similar to a long-playing record, and it has two sides on which data can be stored. Usually the disks are stacked together (10 to 20) on a single rotating spindle. The stack (*disk pack*) is arranged so that each side can be accessed by its own individual playing arm (*seek arm* or *access arm*). Each seek arm is equipped with a *read/write head* (a device which writes data to or reads data from a magnetic recording medium). The computer system maintains an index to the location of particular files on disk, so that the seek arm can move directly to the appropriate access-arm position on the disk,[20] wait for the desired record to rotate beneath the head, and transfer data to or from the file.[21]

The process of locating and transferring data to or from on-line disk storage takes place in thousandths of a second, so that, for the user engaging in *interactive computing*, the process can seem instantaneous.[22] Interactive systems usually allow the use of *Boolean logic* (a method of inquiry that restricts responses to "yes" or "no" and includes logical operators "and," "or," "not," "except," "if," and "then," which may be combined in a variety of ways) in searching a data base (e.g., display the titles of all record series concerning *federal surveillance* "and" the *Students for a Democratic Society* "or" *federal surveillance* "and" the *Black Panther Party* "except" for records of the *Federal Bureau of Investigation*). This type of postcoordinate searching allows the researcher to develop his or her own term relationships or to tailor the response to fit his or her specific needs. Also, the researcher can modify the query in order to broaden or narrow the scope of the search.[23] An archivist using a direct access system can also correct or add data to the file interactively, making current information immediately available.

Archivists considering the respective virtues of direct access systems and sequential access systems may

readily conclude that direct access systems are preferable.[24] Although few would dispute the opinion that direct access systems offer greater capabilities, some archivists feel that direct access is not necessary for archival needs, and thus, the additional expense required to operate these systems is unwarranted. As a general rule, direct access systems are more expensive. The *programming* of direct access is usually more complex, making the acquisition costs greater. In addition, data storage costs in direct access systems are often greater for three reasons: (1) storage space on a magnetic disk costs more than space on magnetic tape or keypunch cards; (2) storage space requirements are usually greater because of additional record control and system indexing data required for random location of the stored records in a direct access system; and (3) the cost to maintain a file on-line for interactive searching is often greater than that for batch processing.[25]

On the other hand, although computer operating costs may be significantly less with some sequential access systems, a direct access system may be simpler and more efficient to operate. The effectiveness of interactive data entry and file editing may lead to lower personnel costs while maintaining a file of higher quality. The ideal data base structure is probably unattainable, but system capabilities and costs must be evaluated in relation to the archival objectives to be accomplished.

The final system feature in this chapter is effective system support, which can be the most important factor in determining the long-term value of any software package. This includes complete and well-written program *documentation* (instructions for use and an explanation of the operation of all programs in the system) and capable and dependable system maintenance and development. The lack of reliable, current documentation limits the transportability of a system from one computer facility to another and will continue to hinder the effective use of the package. Good system maintenance is essential because all newly designed software packages have some errors (*"bugs"*) in them. As these bugs are identified by users, they must be corrected and the documentation appropriately updated. Efforts should be made to improve and expand system capabilities and to communicate notice of these improvements to system users. The most complete and reliable support often comes with those systems owned

---

[20]A single access-arm position is called a *cylinder*.

[21]Davis and McCormack, *The Information Age,* 225-230.

[22]This process is significantly slowed only when many users are simultaneously seeking access to the same data base.

[23]Some direct access systems are designed to conduct complex, Boolean searches in an off-line, batch processing mode, although the interactive mode increasingly predominates.

[24]"Indexed sequential" is a type of direct access file organization which combines the efficiency of sequential organization with the ability to rapidly access records out of sequence from a direct access storage device.

[25]If access is not currently needed, data can be transferred to less expensive off-line disk storage, or can be stored on magnetic tape.

and distributed by well-established computer companies, but these systems are often the most expensive. Large, noncommercial institutions can provide good support if commitment and resource allocation are adequate, or a consortium of users can be organized for cooperation and mutual benefit. Adopting a system without firm and reliable support is a questionable decision, and systems which are dependent on the work or commitment of one individual for maintenance and development should be avoided.[26]

This chapter has been an effort to prepare archivists for making critical examinations and evaluations of the current uses of archival automation. It is also hoped that readers will begin to envision ways and design methods for computer assistance in their own work. The following chapter examines some ways in which archivists are now using computer assistance.

Suggested Readings

Artandi, Susan. *An Introduction to Computers in Information Science*. 2nd ed. Metuchen, N.J.: The Scarecrow Press, Inc., 1972.

Hayes, Robert M., and Becker, Joseph. *Handbook of Data Processing for Libraries*. 2nd ed. Los Angeles: Melville Publishing Company, 1974.

Doyle, Lauren B. *Information Retrieval and Processing*. Los Angeles: Melville Publishing Company, 1975.

3 Archivists and Computers at Work

This chapter examines several computer systems and their current use by archivists. After a cursory introduction to automated information retrieval and a brief review of archival automation during the 1960s, the chapter will survey the use of automation in a number of archival programs during the 1970s. While not comprehensive, this survey intends to convey a sense of what is being done and to illustrate some basic questions concerning archival automation. Systems and applications have been included here because they are representative of various approaches and methods, or because they are indicative of certain difficulties and challenges to be considered in the application of automation in archival repositories. Although some technical description of

each system is included, comparable information is not provided for every system.[27] All of the information here is of recent origin, but with the dynamics of the technology, system modifications and improvements continue to be made. It is a cause for optimism that such changes are taking place.

Automated Information Retrieval

The term *information retrieval* commonly refers to systems or procedures for informing a user of the existence and whereabouts of documents relating to the subject of his or her inquiry.[28] Few information retrieval systems actually retrieve full document texts. Most provide some type of document surrogate, such as a bibliographic citation or a bibliographic citation and a description, or an abstract of document content. The library subject catalog, arranged in classified or alphabetic order, and produced in card or book form, is the most familiar form of information retrieval. Systems such as subject catalogs are *precoordinate* systems because subject relationships are established, once and for all, at the time of cataloging. The user cannot manipulate the subject term or subject class relationships at the time that a search is being conducted. Subject catalogs are also linear in organization. Although a complex subject can be represented by a string of descriptive terms, the entry can be filed only under the initial term, all other terms being subordinate to the first.[29] Multiple access is provided by the creation of duplicate entries with different file locations, but the effort and cost involved determine that the number of entries is limited and that updating is infrequent.[30]

In response to the limitations of the traditional card catalog, systems were developed which allowed a user to manipulate term relationships. During the early 1940s, prior to the invention of electrical computers, optical coincidence systems were developed by W. E. Batten in England and, at the same time, by G. Cordonnier in France. In the Batten and the Cordonnier systems cards were allocated for each descriptive term or document

---

[26]Robert G. Chenhall, *Museum Cataloging in the Computer Age*, 232-233.

[27]Although it is not a purpose of this manual to provide a comparative evaluation of archival automation systems, such a report would be of considerable value to the archival profession.

[28]F. Wilfrid Lancaster, *Information Retrieval Systems: Characteristics, Testing and Evaluation* (New York: John Wiley and Sons, Inc., 1968), 1.

[29]F. Wilfrid Lancaster and Jeanne M. Owen, "Information Retrieval by Computer," *The Information Age: Its Development, Its Impact*, 1-2.

[30]Mike Hyman and Eleanor Wallis, *Mini-Computers and Bibliographic Information Retrieval*, The British Library Research and Development Reports (London: The British Library, 1976), 28.

class. Specific positions on each of these cards were dedicated to each document in the system. Then each document was analyzed and assigned to one or more subject classes, and a hole was punched in the subject card in the position dedicated to the accession number of the document. To retrieve documents relevant to a particular query, the appropriate subject cards could be superimposed, and documents representing the correct combination of subjects could be identified. By adding or subtracting subject cards, one could narrow or broaden the scope of a search. Batten and Cordonnier systems were *postcoordinate indexing* systems, allowing free manipulation of the subject terms, at the time of searching, in order to use whatever logical combinations were appropriate.[31]

A similar postcoordinate system was developed in England in the late 1940s by Calvin Mooers. However, Mooers's system used a different file organization. Whereas Batten and Cordonnier used one card for each term in their vocabularies, Mooers used one card for each document and coded subject terms by notch positions on each card. Mooers's method of organization is now referred to as "item entry" or "term on item," and Batten's method is called "term entry" or "item on term." These are still the two basic methods of organizing index files in modern computer-based information retrieval systems.

A common characteristic of the systems developed by Batten, Cordonnier, and Mooers was their use of *controlled vocabularies* (the use of words or phrases according to a standard list). A controlled vocabulary system is one in which both the indexer and the searcher are limited to sets of terms which appear in an *authority file* (a standard list of terms acceptable for a given function). Controlled vocabularies, commonly exemplified by classification schemes and subject headings lists, had been in routine use for over a hundred years when, in 1951, Mortimer Taube introduced his Uniterm system. Taube's system was the first to use a *natural language* approach (a system in which no vocabulary controls are imposed on the indexing and searching processes).

Taube proposed that, instead of choosing descriptive terms or phrases from an authority file, one could extract single words directly from document text for use as indexing keywords. This proposal received an enthusiastic welcome because it suggested that indexing could be converted to an inexpensive clerical task, but, when applied, the Uniterm approach was often unsatisfactory. A strictly single-word approach was often modified by the use of combined terms. The use of word combination was limited at first, but became quite ex-

tensive. Some information centers, which had adopted single-word indexing, modified their index terms to the point that they began to resemble conventional library subject hearings.[32] The use of single-word indexing soon diminished, and the use of controlled vocabularies returned to dominance. However, the natural language approach had been introduced, and the Uniterm system has had three logical successors: the *keyword in context* (*KWIC*) index, free or full text searching, and automatic indexing.

The basic principle of KWIC, *keyword out of context* (*KWOC*), and other permuted indexing approaches is that words contained in documents, rather than concepts imposed by indexers, can provide effective indexing. Keywords are extracted from a title, abstract, or text and used as indexing terms. In a KWIC index keywords appear in alphabetical order in the context of the words on either side of them, improving their effectiveness as indexing terms.[33] KWIC indexing programs usually include a *stoplist* (a list of minor words, such as prepositions, conjunctions, and articles) containing words which the computer is instructed to ignore in its selection of keywords. The KWIC approach has primarily been used to produce indexes based on the titles of technical or scientific reports and articles. Clearly, the value of a keyword index based on titles is dependent on the degree to which the titles accurately reflect document content.[34]

In using free text or full text systems, the complete texts of all documents are converted to machine-readable form, stored, and searched, dispensing with the need for indexing. In these systems searching is usually done on logical combinations of words occurring in the text, and some systems provide the capacity to specify word distance (how close two or more words must be before they are considered to be related). The legal profession has been the primary user of free text searching, but there has been increasing use of this method in searching scientific texts.[35] This type of information retrieval is quite expensive if the text is not already in machine-readable form, requiring input in full; but text retrieval may become increasingly possible as more texts are being produced in machine-readable form for the purpose of electronic photocomposition.

Automatic indexing is the extraction or assignment of indexing terms directly by computer. From a complete text, text excerpt, or abstract, indexing terms are selected on the basis of certain criteria. Statistical criteria have been applied most often, but linguistic and

[31]Lancaster, *Information Retrieval Systems*, 28-34.

[32]Lancaster and Owen, "Information Retrieval by Computer," 2-8.
[33]In a KWOC index extracted keywords are printed separately in the lefthand margin, with the title in its normal order printed to the right.
[34]Lancaster, *Information Retrieval Systems*, 97-98.
[35]Lancaster and Owen, "Information Retrieval by Computer," 11.

textual criteria have also been used. Typically, the words in a document are listed and statistical measurements are made, often based on the frequency of occurrence of the various words in a document. Words that occurred frequently would be selected as indexing terms for that document, although words with a high frequency in all or most of the documents to be searched would be rejected. Those words would be poor discriminators and would have little indexing value.[36]

There has been a great deal of experimentation with various methods of automatic indexing. The primary objective is to provide indexing as effective as that done manually by highly trained subject specialists, but with significant savings in cost and time. This experimentation has provided useful information concerning the characteristics of effective indexing terms, but there has been relatively little use of this approach in an operational environment.

Although natural language continues to be used in information retrieval, the use of controlled vocabularies has remained prevalent and has grown increasingly sophisticated. The most significant aspect of this growth has been the development and use of the *thesaurus* (a structured, controlled vocabulary which has links from each term to its various associated terms[37]). Evolving from traditional subject headings lists, the first thesaurus created for information retrieval purposes was developed in 1959 by E. I. DuPont de Nemours and Co. Although similar to a conventional list of subject headings, the DuPont thesaurus had an explicit hierarchical and cross-reference structure, and thesaurus terms (*descriptors*) were designed to be combined with other descriptors for both indexing and searching.

Once the thesaurus pattern was established, additional development followed quickly. Within the last twenty years the thesaurus has become the commonly accepted medium of vocabulary control in postcoordinate systems, and now many thesauri exist for a broad range of subject areas.[38]

The evolution of the modern thesaurus is one of many developments which have taken place in the field of information science during the past forty years. Fueled by an urgent need for timely access to a rapidly

growing body of technical and scientific information and by expanding technological capabilities, changes have come quickly. This brief survey of some of the major developments was designed to introduce concepts useful in evaluating the efforts of archivists to improve their methods of intellectual control and access. As archivists examine and evaluate past and present archival uses of automation and consider potential future applications, they are likely to become active participants in the development of modern processes for information storage and retrieval. They should take advantage of the knowledge and experience of other information managers. While archives are unique and neither library cataloging nor science information systems are ideally designed for archival purposes, archivists should not attempt to "reinvent the wheel." All will benefit from the sharing of knowledge, methods, facilities, and ideas.

Early Automation of Archives

The first major effort to use automation in the control of historical documentation was initiated in 1958 in the Manuscript Division of the Library of Congress (LC). The Presidential Papers Section adopted a mechanized approach to the indexing by correspondent of nearly 2,000,000 documents in 23 Presidential collections. The documents were arranged chronologically, and an indexing record was created for each document. Initially, keypunch machines, card sorters, and a tabulator were employed. Each indexing record was limited to the length of an 80-column punched card and consisted of seven fields of information: number identifying the appropriate Presidential collection, writer/recipient, date, series number, page count, additional information, and card count. An eighth field for numbers of subject files or case files was added for three twentieth-century collections, necessitating a reduction in the size of the additional information field. The writer/recipient and date fields were sorted for arrangement of entries in the published indexes.[39]

Although mechanical sorting and listing was superior to manual efforts, it required that each card pass through the sorter twenty-five to thirty times, a noisy and tedious process. When LC acquired a computer in 1964, four programs were written: a shelf-list program, a sort program, an edit program, and a program for producing printer's copy for photo-offset reproduction. When, in 1967, the Linotron, a computerized typesetter, was installed at the Government Printing Office, a fifth program was written to convert the computer output to type characters. Once these pro-

[36]Gerard Salton, *Dynamic Information and Library Processing* (Englewood Cliffs, N.J.: Prentice Hall, Inc., 1975), 77-83.

[37]The five common types of associated terms are: (1) broader terms (less specific), (2) narrower terms (more specific), (3) related terms (at a similar level of specificity with a common broader term), (4) homonymous terms (same term used to describe different subjects), and (5) synonymous terms (different terms used to describe a single subject). The first three are most frequently used, Hyman and Wallis, *Mini-Computers and Bibliographic Information Retrieval*, 28.

[38]Lancaster and Owen, "Information Retrieval by Computer," 8-10.

[39]Russell M. Smith, "Item Indexing by Automated Processes," *American Archivist* 30 (April 1967): 295-302.

grams were in operation, no major changes were made, and the last volume was completed in 1976.[40]

While the punched card format and the 80-character limit proved adequate for producing personal name indexes, item indexing proved very costly and required a great deal of experienced staff time.[41] Budgetary limitations caused reductions in the scale of the project along the way. Full first names were replaced by first and middle initials, and plans for a calendar were canceled. Project costs, excluding all computer costs, which were borne by the Library, have been estimated at one dollar per item.[42] The high price of indexing individual items, chronological arrangement, and limited record length and output formats minimize the applicability of this approach, and the development of two, more sophisticated systems, Master Record of Manuscript Collections (MRMC) and SPINDEX, began in the LC Manuscript Division in the mid-1960s.

MRMC was developed to provide administrative control of the holdings of the Manuscript Division. Selected fields of information were entered for each collection, including title, span and bulk dates, size, shelf location, occupation/function of person or organization, processing status, the presence of restrictions and their lift dates, National Union Catalog of Manuscript Collections (NUCMC) card number, the existence of finding aids or microfilm copies, and statistics of use by readers, requests for photocopying, and circulation by interlibrary loan. In a modified form this system currently provides administrative control and reference statistics for approximately 8,500 collections.

In 1966 it was determined that, in addition to MRMC, an automated system for retrieval of content data should be developed. Experimentation was conducted with KWIC programs and similar word-author index (WADEX) programs. Modification of these produced SPINDEX.

Applying the KWIC approach to archives, existing folder titles can be converted to machine-readable form, and an index of all words in the titles, except stopwords, can be printed. This approach is attractive to archivists because it is similar to traditional folder listings, and the indexing data is easily obtainable; however, this method may not be effective in providing access. Obviously, it is only effective when folder titles actually reflect folder content. This approach is also vulnerable to the vagaries and inconsistencies of natural language use. It would not be appropriate for indexing all of the records in a large repository; nonetheless, it may be adequate for records management purposes or for the records of a single organization.

In the LC Manuscript Division, folder titles, recorded on punched cards, were run through the SPINDEX programs, which printed each word in the titles, except for stopwords, alphabetically. Under each of these keywords, all folder titles in which that keyword appeared were printed, and each title was followed by its container number, abbreviated collection title and collection number.[43]

The capabilities of the original SPINDEX system were severely limited. It provided few data fields, with each limited to about sixty characters. There was no updating or editing capability; corrections could only be made by punching new cards and manually substituting them for the cards in error. There was a limited number of program-generated stopwords; printouts were in uppercase only, and data could only be stored on punched cards. Reprogramming was necessary if the system was to have broad archival application.[44] LC did not develop the system further, but the National Archives and Records Service (NARS) decided to continue SPINDEX development. In order to produce an improved SPINDEX system, NARS requested financial assistance from the Council on Library Resources, Inc., which provided a two-year grant of $40,000. In October 1967, NARS, in cooperation with nine other institutions, began a project to create a system specifically designed to meet archival needs. However, system development proved to be long and arduous; it was not until 1973 that an operational version was available, and system documentation was not published until 1975.[45] This SPINDEX II system is now the most widely used archival automation system in the United States.

While work on the Presidential Papers Project, MRMC, and SPINDEX was proceeding at LC, other repositories were also trying innovative approaches. At the Joseph Downs Manuscript Library of the Henry Francis Du Pont Winterthur Museum, a mechanized, optic-coincidence system, the Termatrex Information Retrieval System, was adopted in 1961.[46] When applied

[40]Marion M. Torchia, "Two Experiments in Automated Indexing: The Presidential Papers and the Papers of the Continental Congress," *American Archivist* 39, 437-440.

[41]John P. Butler, "The Application of Computer Technology to Bibliographic Control of Historical Records" (Paper presented at the Society of American Archivists Conference on Priorities for Historical Records, Chicago, January 6-8, 1977), 7.

[42]Torchia, "Two Experiments in Automated Indexing," 441.

[43]Frank G. Burke, "The Application of Automated Techniques in the Management and Control of Source Materials," *American Archivist* 30 (April 1967): 268-271.

[44]U.S., General Services Administration, National Archives and Records Service, *SPINDEX II, Report and Systems Documentation* (Washington, D.C.: National Archives and Records Service, General Services Administration, 1975), 3.

[45]H. Thomas Hickerson, Joan Winters, and Venetia Beale, *SPINDEX II at Cornell University*, 23-34.

[46]Elizabeth Ingerman Wood, *Report on Project History Retrieval: Tests and Demonstrations of an Optic-Coincidence System of Information Retrieval for Historical Materials,* Drexel Library School Series, No. 14 (Philadelphia: The Drexel Press, 1966), 1-12.

to the small number of manuscripts at the Downs Library, the system proved capable of identifying individual documents containing information relevant to specific inquiries.[47] While simple and inexpensive to operate, this type of mechanical system provides only one type of retrieval process and has no method for storing the results of information searches.

Item indexing was also adopted at the Public Archives of Canada when it began using computer assistance in 1965 to index the papers of Canada's prime ministers. Although similar to the presidential papers project at LC, subject indexing was included, and more sophisticated finding aids were produced: an author index, secondarily sorted by subject, and then by date; a subject index, secondarily sorted chronologically, and then by author; and a chronological index, secondarily sorted by author.[48] The indexing of prime ministers' papers has continued, but high costs led to the abandoning of item indexing in 1970 and the adoption of folder-level indexing.[49]

Also in 1965, the Hoover Institution on War, Revolution and Peace began a pilot project to develop techniques applicable for collections there. In indexing the records of the American Relief Administration, a staff member drew together sets of five to ten documents concerning the same general subject, and created an index record for each set. Indexing keywords were chosen from an authority list which included document types, subject keywords, geographic place names, corporate names, and personal names. Each keyword was limited to 24 characters, and record length was limited to 320 characters. Using IBM 1401 and 7090 computers, an IBM 1401 Library Program provided for the generation and updating of keywords, and the production and searching of tapes to provide selective retrieval in response to specific queries. When printouts were generated, the full 320-character description printed under each keyword.[50] The software-imposed limitation on record and field length and the relatively cumbersome operation of the IBM 1401 computer limited the applicability of this approach. Although the software was later modified to allow 2,200 characters per record, the system has not been applied beyond the records of the American Relief Administration.

Recent Developments in Archival Automation

In the 1960s automated techniques were adopted with considerable optimism, and many archivists expected computer use to be common in major repositories within a decade. This did not happen; early optimism faded, and development slowed. Only in the mid-1970s did archival use of automation expand significantly. It now seems clear that this growth will continue. The development of new systems or new applications of existing systems have become commonplace. The remainder of this chapter describes ten of these systems and their archival applications:

(1) MRMC II (Master Record of Manuscript Collections)

(2) SPINDEX II and III (Selective Permutation INDEXing)

(3) SELGEM (SELf-GEnerating Master)

(4) GRIPHOS (General Retrieval and Information Processing for Humanities-Oriented Studies)

(5) CODOC (COoperative DOCuments)

(6) Corning Glass Works Archives Photonegative Computer Index

(7) ARCHON (ARCHives ON-line)

(8) A system developed for the Survey of Sources for the History of Biochemistry and Molecular Biology

(9) PARADIGM (Programmed Annual Report and Digital Information Generation Matrix)

(10) NARS A-1 (National Archives and Records Service).

The descriptions of these systems and applications are not designed to be comprehensive; instead, the analyses are intended to convey a sense of the scope of current activity, to illustrate various archival approaches to the use of automation, and to identify problems and issues of concern in the implementation of EDP in archives. These descriptions primarily concern single-repository applications; national systems are discussed in Chapter 4.

MRMC II

MRMC II, developed and used by the LC Manuscript Division, is an expanded version of the MRMC system designed for administrative control. After modifying the system several times since its creation in 1967, the staff decided in 1973 that major changes were desirable. Enhancements made possible

---

[47]Elizabeth A. Ingerman, "A New Method of Indexing Manuscripts," *American Archivist* 25 (July 1962): 331-340.

[48]Jay Atherton, "Mechanization of the Manuscript Catalogue at the Public Archives of Canada," *American Archivist* 30 (April 1967): 303-309.

[49]Kenneth W. Duckett, *Modern Manuscripts: A Practical Manual for Their Management, Care and Use* (Nashville, Tenn.: American Association for State and Local History, 1975), 161.

[50]Rita R. Campbell, "Machine Retrieval in the Herbert Hoover Archives," *American Archivist* 29 (April 1966): 298-302.

the production of catalog cards and a cumulative index to the Division's holdings, thus providing access as well as administrative control. These modifications were based on the LC MARC II (MAchine-Readable Cataloging) format (record structure, content, and coding) and were intended to be compatible with the MARC format for manuscripts.[51]

The MARC II format was developed by LC for its own cataloging and for distribution of machine-readable catalog records to be used elsewhere as input for local processing. After the adoption of the MARC II format in 1969, libraries and other subscribing organizations began to receive weekly tapes containing cataloging information for English-language monographs processed that week by LC. The MARC II record for monographs is a variable-length record made up of a combination of fixed and variable-length fields. It is a communication format designed to standardize the creation of machine-readable cataloging records and the transmission of data. The format defines both the content of the cataloging records and the manner in which the data is recorded. The implementation of the MARC project and the distribution of MARC tapes have led to increased standardization in library methodology as libraries have modified their cataloging procedures and their automated systems in order to be compatible with the machine-readable data available from LC.[52]

After the implementation of the MARC II format for monographs, compatible formats for other types of library holdings (e.g., music, serials, and manuscripts) were designed. Unfortunately, the MARC format for manuscripts was created and published without the direct involvement of the LC Manuscript Division.[53] The resulting format was designed primarily for individual item cataloging. Therefore, the "official" MARC format for manuscripts was unacceptable to the Manuscript Division, and its staff created their own unique version of the MARC format. Using their own format on the Library's large Amdahl computers, and operating in a batch processing mode, the Manuscript Division uses MRMC II for all current cataloging, storing and printing catalog entries and indexes created therefrom. However, during 1979 discussions were initiated which may lead to modifications in the Manuscript Division format to achieve compatibility with the MARC format. This would allow the Manuscript Division to use the new on-line catalog system currently being installed at LC.

The MARC manuscripts format is another example of the incompatibility between library individual item cataloging and archival analysis and description. In spite of the potential benefits to be gained from MARC compatibility, the current manuscripts format is not well suited for archival use. Unfortunately, AACR II[54] maintains the individual item approach and seems most appropriate for cataloging literary manuscripts. It now appears that favorable modifications may be made in the MARC manuscripts format and AACR II. Such changes would: (1) be of immediate benefit to the LC Manuscript Division, (2) have an impact on plans to automate NUCMC, and (3) make it possible for archivists to participate in large library networks for transmitting and accessing bibliographic information without unduly sacrificing their own descriptive practices.

SPINDEX II and III

Of all automated systems, archivists are most familiar with SPINDEX. Developed by the National Archives and Records Service (SPINDEX II development was completed in 1974; SPINDEX III became available in 1978), this software is currently used by about two dozen institutions in the United States and Canada. Users include municipal, state, national, church, university, and corporate archives and records management programs. Specific uses range from item indexing of eighteenth-century documents by the South Carolina Department of Archives and History and by NARS, to the production by electronic photocomposition of the National Historical Publications and Records Commission (NHPRC) *Directory of Archives and Manuscript Repositories* (1978), to the indexing of corporate slide presentations by INCO, Limited.

The use of SPINDEX II was initiated at the National Archives in 1969 with the indexing of President John F. Kennedy's White House Subject Files. Since then NARS has used SPINDEX to produce an index to the *Guide to Cartographic Records in the National Archives* (1971), recent finding aids in the series of *Guides to Captured German Records,* the *Catalog of National Archives Microfilm Publications* and the *Index to the Papers of the Continental Congress, 1774-1789* (1978). System use outside the National Archives progressed slowly. Early implementation efforts at the Minnesota Historical Society and the Smithsonian Institution Archives produced unsatisfactory results. It was not until 1973 that two other archival repositories, the South Carolina Department of Archives and History and the

[51]Butler, "The Application of Computer Technology to Bibliographic Control of Historical Records," 3-4.

[52]Susan Artandi, *An Introduction to Computers in Information Science,* 145-150.

[53]U.S., Library of Congress, *Manuscripts: A MARC Format* (Washington, D.C.: Library of Congress, 1973).

[54]Michael Gorman and Paul W. Winkler, eds., *Anglo-American Cataloging Rules,* 2nd ed. (Chicago, Ill.: American Library Association, 1978).

OKLAHOMA

Oklahoma does not have a statewide program for preserving local public records. County and municipal records normally remain in the custody of local officials.

ALVA

OK42-560
Northwestern Oklahoma State University
Library
Alva OK 73717

(405) 327-1700, Ext. 219

OPEN: Su 5-10, M-Th 8-10, F 8-5, Sa 9-noon; closed holidays
and University vacations
COPYING FACILITIES: yes
MATERIALS SOLICITED: Genealogy; local history; and history
of Northwestern Oklahoma State University. Will also accept
other materials.

HOLDINGS:
Total volume: 25 l.f.
Inclusive dates: 1895 -
Description: Materials relating chiefly to Northwestern Oklahoma State University. The collection contains photographs;
correspondence and reminiscences of William J. Mellor and
other alumni; a speech delivered on campus by Eleanor Roosevelt; letters of Ernest Tyler; records of the Sequoyah Children's
Book Award; and University records, 1895-

BARTLESVILLE

OK118-70
Bartlesville Public Library
History Room
6th and Johnstone
Bartlesville OK 74003

(918) 336-2220

OPEN: M-F 9-5, Sa 9-1; closed Sundays and holidays
COPYING FACILITIES: yes
MATERIALS SOLICITED: Biographies of local pioneers. Will also
accept other materials relating to local history or the Delaware
Indians.

HOLDINGS:
Total volume: 7,000 items
Inclusive dates: 1880's -
Description: A collection of manuscripts, photographs, and
lists and rolls relating to the Delaware Indians and to local white
settlers, businesses, and industries in the late 19th and early 20th
centuries.

CLAREMORE

OK245-880
The Will Rogers Memorial
Will Rogers Memorial Library
Office of the Curator
Claremore OK

MAILING ADDRESS:
Box 157
Claremore OK 74017

(918) 341-0719

OPEN: daily 8-5
ACCESS: appointment required
COPYING FACILITIES: yes
MATERIALS SOLICITED: Memorabilia pertaining to the life of
Will Rogers.

HOLDINGS:
Total volume: 6,635 items
Inclusive dates: 1879 - 1935
Description: A collection of manuscripts and visual and audible documents relating to the public and private life of Will
Rogers.

SEE: NUCMC, 1975.

DURANT

OK304-690
Red River Valley Historical Association
Department of Social Sciences
Southeastern Oklahoma State University
Durant OK 74701

(405) 924-0121, Ext. 203

OPEN: M-Sa 9-5; closed Sundays and holidays
ACCESS: permission of president of Association required
COPYING FACILITIES: yes
MATERIALS SOLICITED: History of the Red River Valley, the
American Southwest, and Spanish borderlands, with special attention to Indian tribes.

HOLDINGS:
Total volume: 500 items
Inclusive dates: 1873 -
Description: Materials concerned with early Oklahoma history and the Choctaw and Chickasaw Indians, including tribal
record books and correspondence of Indian chiefs.

Figure 7. Text entries. (Reprinted from the *Directory of Archives and Manuscripts in the United States.* Washington, D.C.: National Historical Publications and Records Commission, 1978, p. 526.)

```
01/16/76           INDEX          PAGE     53

PRES. NO.        SLIDE PRESENTATIONS KEYWORD INDEX

EXPANSION
  N75- 8.05      Shimura Kaku - Tokyo Nickel Expansion Plans,
                   C.E. O'Neill 18/AUG/75
  N75- 8.05      7. Plant Expansion Nickel Oxide Sinter 75,
                   Sulfuric Acid, Nickel Pig
  N75- 8.05      8. Plant Expansion Flowsheet
  N75- 8.05      9. Estimated Capital Costs, Plant Expansion
  N75- 8.05      10. Estimated Operating Costs, Plant Expansion
EXPENDITURE
  N75- 3.06      4. Ease Case Capital Expenditure Assumptions
  N75- 5.10      9. Analysis of 1975 Capital Expenditure
                   Savings
EXPENDITURES
  N75- 4.06      1. Exploration Department - Total Exploration
                   Expenditures
  N75- 4.06      2. Exploration Department - Mines Exploration
                   Expenditures
  N75- 4.06      4. Exploration Department - Field Exploration
                   Expenditures
  N75- 5.10      8. Capital Expenditures
  N75- 6.04      27. Exploration - Forecast Expenditures
  N75- 6.04      28. Exploration - Forecast Expenditures - Field
                   Exploration by Commodities
  N75- 6.04      36. Mines Exploration - Ontario Division
                   Forecast Expenditures
  N75- 9.02      14. Capital Expenditures
  N75- 9.12      14. Capital Expenditures
EXPENSE
  N75- 3.05      2. Ontario Division Operating Expense
  N75- 5.06      2. SG&A Expense
  N75- 5.06      3. Exploration - Research and Development -
                   Interest Expense
  N75- 5.10      6. Expense Analysis - Metals Business - By
                   Class
  N75- 5.10      7. Expense Analysis - Metals Business - By
                   Company
EXPENSES
  N75- 5.06      4. Other Expenses - Freight and Insurance -
                   Other Income
  N75- 5.10      4. Primary Metals and Rolling Mills Cash
                   Operating Expenses - By Class
EXPLANATORY
  N75-10.05      Explanatory Financial Section
EXPLORATION
  N75- 4.06      ESB - Inco Roundtable, W. Steven - Mineral
                   Exploration and New Developments, Skytop, 01 -
                   02/APR/75
  N75- 4.06      1. Exploration Department - Total Exploration
                   Expenditures
```

Figure 8. INCO, Limited, slide presentations index. (Reprinted, by permission, from "Exhibits of INCO, Limited, Applications," in *SPINDEX Users Conference,* ed. H. Thomas Hickerson, p. 110.)

Cornell Department of Manuscripts and University Archives, began to use the system.

The South Carolina Department of Archives and History is currently applying SPINDEX for two purposes. One is the production of a comprehensive series-level descriptive guide similar in content to published inventories of the National Archives. Each series description includes such information as provenance; statutory citations for the creation and changes in the series; description of series content; mention of unusual items of special note; form and arrangement of the series; description of existing indexes and other finding aids; citations for microfilm, transcripts, and publication of the series; and indication of restrictions on access. These descriptions will be printed in hierarchical archival order (i.e., record group, subgroup, series), and a comprehensive index will be included. Initially, this guide will be produced on 16mm computer output microfilm, but, using electronic photocomposition, a letterpress edition may be issued. Unfortunately, the intensive labor required to prepare descriptions for each series has delayed the production of the guide.[55]

While work on the descriptive guide has proceeded slowly, the production of item-level indexes to documents in selected series has progressed steadily. Since July 1973, the staff of the South Carolina Archives has input indexing information for over 100,000 documents or case files. Recently completed is an item-level, consolidated index to 64,000 documents in six series: Land Grants from the Office of the Secretary of State (1694-1776), Judgement Rolls from the South Carolina Court of Common Pleas (1703-1790); Conveyances recorded by the Public Register (1719-1776); Renunciations of Dower from the Court of Common Pleas (1776-1887); and Accounts Audited of Claims Growing Out of the Revolution from the Office of the Comptroller General (1778-1804). This index, produced on five rolls of computer output microfilm, includes 150,000 selected index references to 39,000 different names, locations, and topics.[56] Each index reference is followed by a number identifying the specific document and by a concise abstract of the document.

Very early in their development of computer-assisted indexing techniques, the staff of the South Carolina Archives decided that a controlled vocabulary was necessary for the effective selection of subject, geographic-location, and type-of-document indexing terms. Of these, subject control proved most difficult. Numerous existing subject headings lists, classification schemes, thesauri, and reference works were consulted. None seemed adequate for meeting the particular needs of the South Carolina Archives; so began the difficult task of creating a thesaurus.

The scope, structure, and size of the thesaurus were designed to reflect the nature of particular holdings and the anticipated needs of users of the indexed series. Important subject concepts were identified and defined. Appropriate indexing terms were designated to represent each subject concept. A lead-in vocabulary was created which lists all indexing terms used in the system, and also other possible subject terms which could be used to designate the same concepts. These references lead the user to the designated indexing term; for example, if an indexer or a user is searching for the designated term representing "convict labor" and begins by checking "chain gangs," he will be referred to "convict labor."

In addition to selecting indexing terms and lead-in references, boundaries segregating related subject concepts were defined, and hierarchical and associative relationships for each indexing term were established. Broad, more general terms were cross-referenced to narrow, more specific terms. Narrow terms are often cross-referenced to even more specific terms. Related terms, which are at approximately the same level of specificity,

---

[55] Charles H. Lesser, "Archival Uses of SPINDEX II at the South Carolina Archives," *SPINDEX Users Conference,* ed. H. Thomas Hickerson, 26-31.

[56] "News Notes," *American Archivist* 42 (January 1979): 109.

DATES	TITLE	SER	BOX	FLD	LVL	TYPE	COLL ID	REPOS
INDEX 06/04/73 PAGE 889								
WATERMAN WILLIAM T								
1946-1948	ROT- ROW- ROY-	1	47	47	4	CORR C-RF	03/06/0008	COR
WATERMARGIN INC								
1946-1950	WAT- WAY-	1	54	99	4	CORR C-RF	03/06/0008	COR
WATERS THOMAS E								
1948-1950	THI DELTA CHI	1	52	70	4	CORR	03/06/0008	COR
WATERTOWN DAILY NEWS								
1943-1945	RUSSIAN: CONTEMPORARY RUSSIAN CIVILIZATION SEE ALSO - ROCKEFELLER FOUNDATION	1	11	20	4	CORR ARTL RPT	03/06/0008	COR
WATKINS EXPRESS								
1938	WAT- WAY-	1	57	2	4	CLP	03/06/0008	COR
WATKINS FREDERICK M								
1945-1948	GOVERNMENT MISCELLANEOUS	1	7	60	4	CORR	03/06/0008	COR
WATKINS RALPH J								
1939-1950	AMERICAN STATISTICAL ASSOCIATION	1	5	25	4	CORR	03/06/0008	COR
WATSON GOODWIN								
1943-1945	POST-WAR PLANNING	1	45	94	4	CORR NLTR ARTL CLP	03/06/0008	COR
WATSON JOHN C								
1946	FREEDOM AND THEN WHAT? COMMENCEMENT JUNE 23, 1946 SCHOELLKOPF FIELD	1	58	89	4	CORR MAGZ SPCH	03/06/0008	COR
1947	RETAIL MERCHANTS	1	47	11	4	CORR	03/06/0008	COR
WATSON LABORATORIES								
1937-1950	EI	1	18	16	4	CORR C-RF	03/06/0008	COR
WATSON THOMAS J								
1940-1945	NATIONAL A -	1	39	16	4	FRCD RPT LIST CORR	03/06/0008	COR
1940-1945	MEX- MEY-	1	38	48	4	CORR C-RF	03/06/0008	COR
1941-1942	END	1	18	22	4	CORR	03/06/0008	COR
1946-1949	INTERNATIONAL BUSINESS MACHINES	1	27	27	4	CORR	03/06/0008	COR
1946-1950	WAT- WAY-	1	54	99	4	CORR C-RF	03/06/0008	COR
1950	VASSAR COLLEGE	1	54	13	4	CORR MINS	03/06/0008	COR
WATTERS HAROLD J								
1945	ROTC AND AIR FORCES	1	47	6	4	CORR	03/06/0008	COR
WATTLES THOMAS L								
1947-1949	ROTC - NAVAL	1	47	4	4	CORR	03/06/0008	COR
WATUMULL ELLEN J								
1944-1948	WATUMULL FOUNDATION	1	54	98	4	CORR RLSE NLTR PAMP	03/06/0008	COR
1948-1950	GN-	1	60	26	4	CORR C-RF	03/06/0008	COR
WATUMULL FDN								
1944-1948	WATUMULL FOUNDATION	1	54	98	4	CORR RLSE NLTR PAMP	03/06/0008	COR
1948-1950	GN-	1	60	26	4	CORR C-RF	03/06/0008	COR

Figure 9. Collection index. (Reprinted, by permission, from Hickerson et al., "Guide to the Edmund Ezra Day Papers, 1921-1952," in *SPINDEX II at Cornell,* p. 88.)

are cross-referenced. Indexers are generally instructed to select the most specific terms applicable, and the thesaurus reflects the greatest degree of specificity in those areas in which holdings are most extensive. The thesaurus is modified frequently. As new record series are indexed, new terms are added after careful review.[57] While this thesaurus was developed for indexing a diverse range of historical documents, it has been closely tailored to suit the holdings of the South Carolina Archives, and for indexing individual documents. As a result, large portions of it are not applicable to the archives of other states. It is also unlikely that such extensive indexing of individual documents will be adopted by many other repositories, but the staff of the South Carolina Archives feel that the nature and the quantity of their user demand both justify and necessitate this approach.[58]

The initial venture into the use of EDP by the Cornell University Department of Manuscripts and University Archives was the production of a finding aid for the papers of a Cornell University president. The "Guide to

the Edmund Ezra Day Papers, 1921-1952" (1975) includes narrative descriptions of collection and series content, and a folder-level alphabetical index containing subject, personal name, and organization keywords (single words or phrases). Under each keyword, related folder titles are listed chronologically by the span dates for folder contents. Information printed for each folder includes: full folder title; series, box, and folder numbers; hierarchical level number (which indicates that the unit described is a folder rather than a collection, series, box, or item); physical or intellectual record types contained within the folder; collection identification number; and repository identification. The index was produced in 922 standard printout pages (11-by-14½-inch) and divided into four segments in order to assist handling.

This finding aid substantially improved access to this large collection, but the project staff was overly inclusive in their use of indexing terms, especially in the case of highly specific subject terms. Term use was standardized without a controlled vocabulary. As a result 11,359 different indexing terms were used. Approximately 40 percent of these were subject terms, many of which were used only once. Thus, the index entries are very precise, but a researcher may be required to search under several different keywords to locate a substantial

[57]Sharon G. Avery, "Subject Access through SPINDEX II at the South Carolina Archives" (Paper presented at the forty-first Annual Meeting of the Society of American Archivists, Salt Lake City, October 4-7, 1977).

[58]Lesser, "Archival Uses of SPINDEX II at the South Carolina Archives," 28-31.

portion of the folders relevant to his or her inquiry. This problem may be aggravated by the precoordinate nature of SPINDEX-generated indexes since the system does not allow a researcher to search the data base using term relationships which differ from those established by the indexer.[59]

The Department of Manuscripts and University Archives has continued to use SPINDEX II to produce finding aids for individual and related archival and manuscript collections. Adding geographic location to standard descriptors and using a more controlled vocabulary, they have continued their initial approach. However, the same types of descriptors are not necessarily used throughout a collection. Usually decisions are made on a series basis depending on the nature and access needs of each series. Nor is the same unit for description always used throughout a collection. Some series can be more appropriately controlled at the series, box, or item level. Although the descriptive approach is consistent, an effort is made to retain the flexibility necessary for archival arrangement and description.

SPINDEX II has also been used at Cornell to produce bibliographic access for university publications, including print and near-print items in the archives which have been published or issued by a university unit or the content of which relates to Cornell.[60] Currently, an archival acquisitions system is being developed which will allow for the printing of monthly accession reports, annual and cumulative accessions lists, and a donor list from the same bibliographic record.

Perhaps the most ambitious, completed project using SPINDEX II concerns the conversion to machine-readable form of the card catalog to the holdings of the Historical Branch of the Church of Jesus Christ of Latter-day Saints (LDS). The new catalog consists of a guide and an index, both printed on white printout paper which has been burst, trimmed, and placed in binders. The guide is a formatted list in call number order of all cataloged collections, including main entry, title, collection number, and a content note. The index is an alphabetical list of main entries and subjects with appropriate titles and collection numbers appearing under each keyword. The index refers the researcher to the guide where, by reading the content note, he can learn more about the collection. The initial guide included 4,677 records on 613 pages; the index contained 11,989 individual entries on 391 pages. The guide and index are produced from the same master file, and several special lists, including lists of journals and diaries, non-English language materials, daugerreo-

types, restricted materials, and donors, are also created from the same bibliographic records.[61] Through these multiple uses of the same data base, EDP offers opportunities for considerable cost savings while improving bibliographic control and access.

The basic SPINDEX II programs provide for the printing of a register (a formatted, narrative collection description or abstract) and an index. The index provides for a primary sort of keywords, alphabetically or chronologically, and a secondary sort by either title or date. In addition to printouts, computer output microfilm has been produced at the South Carolina Archives and computer output microfiche by LDS. NARS has created special interface programs that use the photocomposition capabilities of the Government Printing Office (GPO) Linotron 1010. However, after the staff of the NHPRC decided to use SPINDEX in the creation of a national data base of information on archives and manuscripts in the United States,[62] they requested that NARS make significant changes in the SPINDEX II software package. Carrying out these modifications resulted in the creation of SPINDEX III.

SPINDEX III software now consists of four programs from SPINDEX II (ARSP1A through ARSP4 input and file maintenance programs, programmed in IBM Assembler Language) and seven new programs (SPIN3PA through SPIN3PG, programmed in COBOL). The changes were primarily designed to facilitate the use of electronic photocomposition and to improve the indexing capabilities, including greater flexibility and a tertiary sort capacity.[63] These enhancements, in addition to improvements in file-processing efficiency and providing a program for selective extraction of records from the master file, were completed in 1978.

In addition to the creation of SPINDEX III, the decision by the NHPRC to create a national data base has also led to the initiation of a number of NHPRC-funded projects to gather and contribute SPINDEX data to the NHPRC data base. The first of these projects, a comprehensive statewide survey of historical records in the state of Washington, began in April 1977. There are now about a half-dozen cooperating state survey projects and a project involving four state archives in the Midwest. As a condition of funding, these

[59]Hickerson, Winters, and Beale, *SPINDEX II at Cornell*, 35-49.

[60]H. Thomas Hickerson, "A Control System for University Publications," *Documentation Newsletter* 3 (Fall 1977), 8-10.

[61]Brent G. Thompson, "SPINDEX II as a Card Catalog Replacement in the LDS Church Archives," *SPINDEX Users Conference,* ed. H. Thomas Hickerson, 58-61.

[62]Larry J. Hackman, Nancy Sahli, and Dennis A. Burton, "The NHPRC and a Guide to Manuscript and Archival Materials in the United States," *American Archivist* 40 (April 1977): 201-205.

[63]Stephen Hannestad, "SPINDEX III," *SPINDEX Users Conference,* ed. H. Thomas Hickerson, 67-70.

projects have agreed to create machine-readable bibliographic records which are compatible with NHPRC's national data base design, including standard information elements, a prescribed tag structure, and standard codes, such as photocomposition commands. In addition to contributing to the NHPRC national guide project, all of these projects have their own unique purposes and will create products which meet their own goals.[64]

SPINDEX has also been used for records management purposes by several organizations, including IN-CO; Steel Company of Canada; Coca-Cola; City of Portland, Oregon; and the Pacific Northwest Public Power Records Survey. Do archivists make widespread use of SPINDEX because it is an ideal archival automation system? Clearly, the answer is no, but SPINDEX does have a number of system characteristics which are particularly appropriate for archival use:

(1) Variable-length records, variable-length fields, and variable-occurrence fields permit the use of the system to describe and index different types of documentation in varying degrees of detail and for different purposes.

(2) The maximum record length of 7,000 characters, with a potential of up to fifty fields of up to 986 characters each, is sufficient for almost all archival uses.

(3) Machine-generated and/or assigned indexing terms may be used.

(4) The hierarchical level indicator allows the same indexing pattern to be used for accessing and associating different archival control levels, e.g., record group, series, folder.

(5) Low operating cost permits the production of inexpensive line printer-generated or COM listings. After entering the data, the cost of producing the new LDS catalog, including generating and updating the master file and producing the guide and the index, was $100.85.[65]

An additional factor encouraging SPINDEX use is the existence of an organized users group, SPINDEX Users' Network (SUN), which can provide assistance and cooperation in system use and development.[66]

At least four additional factors not directly related to system effectiveness have contributed to the growth of SPINDEX use:

(1) Of the small body of literature directly pertaining to archival automation in the United States and Canada, about half concerns SPINDEX.

(2) During the last three years the NHPRC has increased the number of SPINDEX users by its use of SPINDEX compatibility as a determining factor in allocation of public funds for archival support.

(3) The cost of purchasing the SPINDEX programs from NARS (SPINDEX II, $500 and SPINDEX III, $1500 for nonprofit institutions) is very low.

(4) Since 1978, software purchasers have been provided the opportunity to attend a NARS SPINDEX III Users Training Course.

While there are real advantages to SPINDEX, certain factors limit its use. SPINDEX is not a sophisticated system; it lacks many of the "niceties" which we normally expect of modern information retrieval systems. Error messages (messages notifying the user he has made an error or indicating why an application will not run as entered) are few and ambiguous. Most major system users have programmed their own data entry routines because of the inadequacies of the existing input routines. Existing methods for editing and updating the master file are antiquated. Although the system was designed to facilitate user control of output creation, uncorrected bugs in the software limit this capacity. Ease of system operation is also limited by inadequacies in system documentation. SPINDEX II documentation contains some significant inaccuracies, and SPINDEX III system documentation is not yet available. All of these problems can be, to some degree, attributed to the fact that NARS has been a less-than-ideal source of system maintenance and development. While there has been considerable improvement in the last few years, the level of NARS support has fluctuated during the past decade. This problem and the associated difficulties are to some degree mitigated by the existence of an organized group of

[64]Nancy Sahli, "SPINDEX: A Computer Tool for Subject and Name Access" (Paper presented at the Annual Meeting of the American Library Association, Dallas, June 24, 1979), 6-8.

[65]Thompson, "SPINDEX II as a Card Catalog Replacement in the LDS Church Archives," 59.

[66]SUN membership is open to individuals and organizations with an interest in SPINDEX and archival automation. Individual membership (adjunct: $10.00 per year) entitles one to receive SUN: The

Newsletter of the SPINDEX Users' Network, technical notes, and other publications and to attend all SUN meetings. Institutional membership ($75.00 per year, limited to system users) entitles organizations to program modifications and new programs which have been made available by other SUN members for the cost of tape duplication only. This sharing of programs is very important because several SUN members have produced program modifications which significantly enhance the basic SPINDEX package, but even more important is the existence of a group of experienced system users who are firmly committed to mutual assistance.

RETENTION POLICY SCHEDULE BY DEPARTMENT
04/20/76   PAGE 7

ACCT N-AC   CONTINUED

TITLES	RS #	LOC	D	C	RC	OFF	RC	T	START-TERM	REMARKS
Purchase Journal Entries	N1314	NYO	X		X	2	5	7		Review with Tax Section Before Destruction
Purchase Orders	N1388	NYO	X	X						Sub-Schedule
Reference Individual Reference Files	N1300	NYO	X	X						
Reference Section Reference Files	N2031	NYO	X							Sub-Schedule
Renegotiation Act	N1346	NYO	X	X	X	1	6	7		
Retirement System - Cancelled Checks	N1775	NYO	X	X	X					
Retirement System - Mortgage Files	N2793	NYO	X	X	X					
Retirement System Files	N2808	NYO	X	X	X					
Retirement System Ledger	N2775	NYO	X	X	X					
Retirement System Normal Provision	N1389	NYO	X	X	X					
Royalty Files	N1295	NYO	X	X		5	5			
Sales	N1434	NYO	X	X						
Sales Registers - Miscellaneous Customers	N1679	NYO	X	X						
Section Reference Material	N2025	NYO	X			P				Manuals, Duplicate Set Year End Inventories Plant Chart of Accts GGH - Govt Contracts
Securities Statements	N1787	NYO	X	X						
Security Advices - Corporate	N1390	NYO	X	X						
Sickness & Disability Records with Bank Reconciliation & Cancelled Checks & Vouchers	N1536	NYO	X	X						
Sickness Disability Cash Book	N1950	NYO	X	X	X	6mo	2.5	3		
Source Data Customer Sales Orders-Completed	N1656	NYO	X	X		1	1	1		
Source Data Daily Advice of Shipments	N1683	NYO	X	X		4				
Source Data Drawback Prices	N2028	NYO	X					X		
Source Data Invoices	N1298	NYO	X	X		1	5	6		Review by Senior Sales Acct Before Destruction
Source Data Summary of Shipments and Receipts	N2019	NYO	X			C+1	C+1			Inco Inc & Inco Canada Excluding HAPD Royalties
Special Costs & Statistics	N2023	NYO	X	X		P				Inco Canada
Special Order Expenditure Statements	N1677	NYO	X	X						Sub-Schedule
Special Order Expenditures	N1485	NYO	X			C+2	C+2			
Special Order Requisitions	N1486	NYO	X	X		T	15	T+15		
Specimen File	N1424	NYO	X			5	5			
Statutory Account for Mond and Subsidiaries	N1391	NYO								Blank Forms

Figure 10. INCO, Limited, Retention Policy Schedule by Department. (Reprinted, by permission, from "Exhibits of INCO, Limited, Applications," in *SPINDEX Users Conference*, ed. H. Thomas Hickerson, p. 107.)

users, but adequate, stable system support has yet to be established.

System characteristics which limit the range of SPINDEX application include:

(1) Hardware dependence. Since it is partially programmed in IBM Assembler Language, it will operate only on IBM 360/370 computers.

(2) Records are incompatible with MARC.

(3) Lack of arithmetic capabilities.

(4) Sequential access, batch processing, requirements. SPINDEX data bases cannot be searched in an interactive mode using Boolean operators, and its sequential access storage pattern severly limits it potential efficiency for use as an on-line data base.

SELGEM

SELGEM is a package of computer programs developed for use by museums for general information processing, including collection documentation and cataloging and related research-oriented projects. Developed by the Information Systems Division of the Smithsonian Institution, it is one of the two most widely used systems for museum cataloging in the United States. SELGEM is currently being used to maintain and process curatorial, bibliographic, archival and registration data for several types of collections.

SELGEM consists of approximately 25 basic programs designed for batch processing. A SELGEM master file can be searched on the basis of multiple variables in conjunction with Boolean operators. The system, programmed in COBOL, was developed on Honeywell computer equipment, but has been successfully adapted to operate on other types of computers including the Control Data 6400 and 3100, IBM 360/30 and 40, Univac 1106 and 1110, and GE 625.[67] While a computer system may operate effectively at the institution where it was created, the same system may not be easily installed elsewhere, even on similar equipment, because of sloppy programming, poor system documentation, or differences in the operating systems at various computer centers. Of the systems currently being used by archivists, only SELGEM has run successfully on a variety of equipment.

Although museum cataloging is oriented towards the control of single items, SELGEM has been adapted for archival use by the Smithsonian Institution Archives

to generate a name index, subject index, and a combination name-subject index to each collection. Specialized indexes concerning specific subject areas can also be produced from the same data.

These finding aids to collections are primarily used to provide folder-level access, but references to individual documents or to larger units are often included in the same index. Questions concerning indexing guidelines have arisen in this application. For example, should institutional names be included with personal names in the name index or included in the subject index? Subject indexing has developed without structured guidelines. The feasibility of constructing a subject thesaurus is being investigated.

The other major use of computer assistance by the Smithsonian Archives has been in the production of a comprehensive guide to their holdings. In 1975 the Archives decided to publish a revised edition of its 1971 guide, using EDP, which allows for more frequent and less costly revisions. The Archives also hopes to use COM to produce updated copies between published editions. The information elements and the field structure were designed to produce a guide very similar to the 1971 guide. The main text, excluding table of contents, preface, introduction, appendixes, and index, was printed by the GPO Linotron 1010.[68] This guide, *Guide to the Smithsonian Archives* (Washington, D.C.: Smithsonian Institution Press), was published in 1978. The archives staff has indicated that the use of automation significantly increased the cost of producing this edition, but, now that the data is in machine-readable form, future editions can be updated and produced quickly and at less cost.

The SELGEM program package and system documentation are provided without charge to noncommercial institutions. It is a well-documented system, and personnel of the Smithsonian Office of Computer Services will provide limited assistance to system users by telephone and mail. A system users' group called Museum Exchange for SELGEM Help (MESH) publishes a newsletter. MESH members help each other in the use of SELGEM, but MESH is not designed to assist in new installations. Experience indicates that SELGEM implementation on equipment other than Honeywell may cost approximately $5,000.[69]

---

[67]Chenhall, *Museum Cataloging in the Computer Age,* 93-117.

[68]Alan L. Bain, "Computer Applications to Archives and Manuscripts at the Smithsonian Institution Archives," *ADPA* 2, 13-21.

[69]Chenhall, *Museum Cataloging in the Computer Age,* 117-120.

		DATE	RECORD UNIT	LOCATION
00279400	CENTURY COMPANY			
	REFERRED TO BY LYMAN B. STURGIS	1921– 1922	SIA7075	CD4.86.F11
00279500	CHADWICK, W. A.	09/22/1898	SIA7075	CD1.91.F4
00279600	CHITTENDEN, RUSSELL H.			
	SEE UNDER SMITHSONIAN INSTITUTION BOARD OF REGENTS			
00279700	CHRISTOPHER, ALICE HERRING	11/26/1906	SIA7075	CD4.86.F10
00279700	CHRISTOPHER, JOSEPH	1918– 1919	SIA7075	CD4.05.F3
00279700	CHRISTOPHER PUBLISHING HOUSE	1918– 1919	SIA7075	CD4.05.F3
00279800	CLAPP, GEORGE H.	1918– 1919	SIA7075	CD4.05.F3
00279900	CLARK, JOHN.B.	1890– 1919	SIA7075	CD1.81.F5
	SEE UNDER SMITHSONIAN INSTITUTION BOARD OF REGENTS			
00280000	CLARK, WILLIAM PECKHAM	11/22/1906	SIA7075	CD4.86.F10
00280100	COLLIER, WILLIAM MILLER	1921	SIA7075	CD4.95.F4
00280200	COMMITTEE OF ONE HUNDRED	03/24/1922	SIA7075	CD4.85.F4
	REFERRED TO BY IRVING FISHER			
00290600	CONCHOLOGY	1906	SIA7075	CD4.85.F7
00280300	CONGRESSIONAL CLUB	1890–1923	SIA7075	CD4.85.F4
00290600	CUBA	1906–1923	SIA7075	CD4.85.F4
00290600	EXPEDITION (1914)	1890–1923	SIA7075	
00290600	FRESH WATER SHELLS	1890–1923	SIA7075	
00290600	LAND SHELLS	1890–1923	SIA7075	
00290600	POLITICAL AFFAIRS	1890–1923	SIA7075	
00280300	CULLOM, SHELBY MOORE	1906–1923	SIA7075	CD4.85.F4
00280400	DALL, WILLIAM H.	11/07/1907	SIA7075	CD1.01.F6
00280500	DALZELL, JOHN	NO DATE AVAILABLE	SIA7075	CD4.05.F5
00290600	DANA, EDWARD SALISBURY			
	SEE UNDER SMITHSONIAN INSTITUTION BOARD OF REGENTS			
00280800	DE FOREST, HENRY SCHERMERHORN	11/29/1906	SIA7075	CD4.86.F10
00281000	DE SIBOUR, J. H.	03/19/1907	SIA7075	CD4.85.F5
00280900	DE SIBOUR, J. H.	1920– 1921	SIA7075	CD4.85.F5
00280700	DEAN, A.	07/30/1921	SIA7075	CD1.81.FG
00280700	DEAN, BASHFORD	1894– 1921	SIA7075	CD1.01.FG
00281100	DRAKE, C. M.	1894– 1921	SIA7075	CD1.81.FG
00281200	ELIOT, C. E.	01/11/1900	SIA7075	CD1.01.FG
00281300	ELKIN, W. L.	1899– 1900	SIA7075	CD1.81.FG
	SEE UNDER SMITHSONIAN INSTITUTION BOARD OF REGENTS			
00290600	EXPEDITION TO	11/17/1906	SIA7075	CD4.86.F10
	CUBA			
00290600	EXPEDITIONS TO	1890– 1923	SIA7075	
	BAHAMA ISLANDS	1890– 1923	SIA7075	
00290600	HAITI	1890– 1923	SIA7075	
00290600	JAMAICA	1890– 1923	SIA7075	
00281400	FAIRBANK, CHARLES WARREN	1906– 1912	SIA7075	CD4.05.F6
00281400	FARQUHAR, A. B.	1906– 1912	SIA7075	CD4.85.F6
00281500	FAUNCE, WILLIAM HENRY PERRY			
	SEE UNDER SMITHSONIAN INSTITUTION BOARD OF REGENTS			
00281600	FISHER, IRVING	11/30/1906	SIA7075	CD4.86.F10
00281700	FISKE, THOMAS S.	1906– 1907	SIA7075	CD4.05.F7
	SEE UNDER SMITHSONIAN INSTITUTION BOARD OF REGENTS			
00290600	FLORIDA	11/28/1906	SIA7075	CD4.86.F10
00290600	DREDGING EXPEDITION	1890– 1923	SIA7075	

Figure 11. Name-subject index to the Henderson Family Papers, Record Unit #7075. (Reprinted, by permission from Bain, "Computer Applications to Archives and Manuscripts at the Smithsonian Institution Archives," p. 17.)

(7075)

Henderson Family Papers, 1868-1923
(2.7 cubic feet).

John Brooks Henderson (1826-1913), a lawyer and politician, served as United States Senator from Missouri from 1862 to 1869. In 1869, he returned to St. Louis where he practiced law and remained active in both local and national politics. In 1889, he retired from practice and moved to Washington, D. C. From 1892 to 1911, he served as a citizen member of the Smithsonian Institution Board of Regents.

Henderson's wife, Mary Foote Henderson (1841-1931), was involved in the suffrage and temperance movements. She was also a well-known socialite in Washington and a devotee of the arts, as well as an author of children's books and books on health.

John Brooks Henderson, Jr. (1870-1923), the son of John Brooks and Mary Foote Henderson, graduated from Harvard University in 1891, and Columbian Law School (now George Washington University) in 1893. From 1896 to 1897, Henderson was secretary to John W. Foster, a diplomatic advisor to the Chinese government. In 1897, he travelled with General Nelson A. Miles on a tour of Europe and the Ottoman Empire as a civilian observer of the armies of the great European powers. He was appointed a citizen member of the Smithsonian Institution Board of Regents in 1911 and retained that post until his death. Interested in shell collecting as a youth, Henderson later concentrated on the marine shell life of the West Indies and participated in several expeditions to the Caribbean. His collections were donated to the United States National Museum. He did volunteer work in the Division of Mollusks in his spare time, and wrote several articles for the *Proceedings of the United States National Museum*, and *Bulletin of the United States National Museum*. He was also the author of *American Diplomatic Questions*, 1901, and *The Cruise of the Tomas Barrera*, 1916, based on his expedition to Cuba in 1914.

The Henderson Family papers contain John Brooks Henderson, Jr.'s correspondence; literary manuscripts; scientific notebooks; lists of shells from the Caribbean, Maine, and North Carolina; Henderson family correspondence, including John Brooks Henderson, Jr.'s correspondence describing his travels; correspondence concerning the endorsement of Irving Fisher for Secretary of the Smithsonian Institution; cancelled checks; appointment calendars; medical and real estate records; notes; genealogy; Mary Foote Henderson's recipe and guest books; records from the United States Treasury Department on imports and exports; immigration and population statistics; federal expenditure statistics, 1892-1893; photographs, some of which were taken by Matthew Brady; blueprints; architectural drawings; newspapers; and journal articles.

ARRANGEMENT: (1) John Brooks Henderson, Jr., general correspondence, 1892-1923; (2) John Brooks Henderson, Jr., literary manuscripts and description of Haiti; (3) John Brooks Henderson, Jr., scientific notebooks, logbook, and manuscripts, 1899-1914; (4) Henderson family, general correspondence, 1868-1923; (5) Henderson family, genealogy, appointment calendars, medical reports, fiscal and real estate records, blueprints, and drawings; (6) Henderson family, guest books, recipe books, notes, pamphlets, journal, newspaper articles, and photographs. FINDING AIDS: Description in control file.

Figure 12. Guide entry for the Henderson Family Papers, Record Unit #7075. (Reprinted, by permission, from *Guide to the Smithsonian Archives*. Washington, D.C.: Smithsonian Institution Press, 1978, p. 194-195.)

GRIPHOS

Another automated system widely used by museums in the United States is GRIPHOS, a general purpose system, including approximately thirty programs in the basic package. These programs perform a broad variety of functions, including input, editing, file correction, indexing, vocabulary analysis, selective retrieval, report generation, and transmission of data to other programs for statistical analysis or other purposes. Each program contains a set of parameters which allows the user to alter the function of the programs; for example, a retrieval program can be directed to select certain data categories for inclusion in a catalog report, and might be modified by a different set of parameters to retrieve data and produce catalog cards.[70]

GRIPHOS was developed over a ten-year period at a cost of approximately $500,000 by Jack Heller, a computer science professor at the State University of New York (SUNY) at Stony Brook, where it is currently maintained. It was developed and initially used for library bibliographic record keeping at the United Nations Library, but in 1967 the system became associated with a developing consortium of American art museums in New York and Washington, the Museum Computer Network, Inc. (MCN). Since 1968, the system has been used most widely by art museums for maintaining catalog files, biography files, and film library files, but it is also being used for intellectual control of historical photograph collections at the Photographic Archive of the Yale Center for British Art and at the International Museum of Photography at George Eastman House.

MCN is a nonprofit corporation, composed of museums and organizations cooperating in the conversion of collection-related records to machine-readable form. In carrying out this conversion, MCN seeks to achieve as much uniformity and compatibility among users as the diverse nature of museum collections permits.[71] Intending that data generated by network members will be both technologically and conceptually compatible, MCN has, from its formation, sought both technical and intellectual conformity in the use of the GRIPHOS system.

MCN markets and supports GRIPHOS and is the sole system distributor to museums. System users must be active members of MCN ($250 annual membership fee) and pay an additional annual subscription fee of $750 in order to receive the programs. Subscribers also receive system documentation and technical assistance. Users are not permitted to make program modifications, but all members receive updated versions of the system and the documentation when enhancements are developed at Stony Brook. MCN provides guidelines for data field use, precisely defining the descriptive elements to be used so that all users apply the same tag numbers to mean approximately the same thing.[72] Rigorous in approach, MCN has sought to bring conformity to an area which, like archives, has been traditionally characterized by nonconformity.

The GRIPHOS programs are written in PL/1, a language primarily used on IBM equipment, and are compiled into machine language using the IBM OS/360 operating system. Therefore, the system operation is limited to medium and large members of the IBM 360 and 370 series or to the RCA Spectra, using OS. GRIPHOS data files are organized and structured for processing on direct access file storage devices. Searches of GRIPHOS files can be conducted using a variety of logical operators. GRIPHOS was designed to operate in a batch processing mode but current plans include the development of terminal-operated, on-line operation for parts of the system.[73]

CODOC

CODOC is an automated system used by the COoperative DOCuments Project of the Ontario Universities' Library Cooperative System (OULCS) to process and retrieve government documents. It has also been used to produce a printed catalog, *Regional Collection, The D.B. Weldon Library, Catalogue,* (London, Ontario: University of Western Ontario, 1977) to *Municipal Records* (vols. I and II) and *Personal Manuscripts* (vol. III) in the Regional Collection of the University of Western Ontario. The development of CODOC for government documents represents a recognition by several libraries that conventional library classification and cataloging procedures are not necessarily the most appropriate method for controlling all types of published materials. The Cooperative Documents Project has adopted an archival approach which is less expensive and more effective for control and access to published government documents.

Seeking to devise a system for processing and retrieving government publications which caters to the special characteristics of governmental agencies and the special access needs of document users, the University of Guelph, Ontario, created the Guelph Documents

---

[70]*Ibid.,* 120-121.
[71]*Museum Computer Network, Inc.* (Stony Brook, N.Y.: Museum Computer Network, Inc., 1976).

[72]Chenhall, *Museum Cataloging in the Computer Age,* 243.
[73]*Ibid.,* 122-148.

System in 1967. Initially, the system was used jointly by the University of Guelph and the University of Western Ontario, but, in 1972, ownership, operation, and further development was transferred to the OULCS Documents Project. At present, the system is being used by fifteen libraries in Ontario and Quebec. CODOC is used as an in-house system by each library; but similar procedures, including the same coding manual, forms, and computer programs, are used at all libraries, and their records are contributed monthly to a common data base from which a cumulative union shelf list is produced biannually. A title listing, an index to corporate authors and series appearing on the union shelf list, and monthly supplements to the union list, are also produced from this data base.

Using a single, unified arrangement and coding scheme, each library is capable of handling documents from any agency in any country. The coding scheme is tied to the main entry (agency of origin), and, unlike library classification, is not designed to reflect the subject content of the document. The coding is based on governmental jurisdictions, levels of government, and issuing agency. This information can be taken directly from the title page by clerical staff, and the publications are physically arranged by the same scheme, offering a valuable browsing capacity to the user. The library user may also search the collection by using any one of six catalogs produced in-house by the system: corporate author, individual author, title, series, serial, and a KWOC index designed to provide subject access. Keywords in the KWOC index are derived from publication titles and can be enriched by adding a limited number of additional subject descriptors. The effectiveness of the KWOC index is largely dependent on the relevance of the document titles. Since government reports ususally concern current research and titles use contemporary terminology, access through the KWOC index is probably superior to LC subject headings.[74]

The CODOC record format includes fixed-length and variable-length fields. The fixed-length fields include document numbers, language, library, frequency of publication, and document type. Bibliographic data is contained in 80-column (character) segments; the largest variable-length field has a maximum length of nine, 80-column segments (720 characters); and the maximum, total record length is fifteen segments (1,200 characters). Most members of OULCS and the union portion of the system use CODOC in a batch mode; however, the University of Toronto, the Canadian Department of External Affairs, and the Ecole Polytechnique in Montreal use programs developed by the University of Toronto Library for on-line input and editing. The University of Toronto concluded that CODOC and MARC were largely compatible. Although there is not always a one-to-one relationship, CODOC to MARC translation procedures have been established, and CODOC records can now be integrated into the total bibliographic data base of the University of Toronto Library.[75]

The Regional Collection of the D.B. Weldon Library at the University of Western Ontario began in the 1920s as a small, informal repository, acquiring a few manuscript records belonging to prominent local families. Gradually, a systematic collection development strategy evolved. Records of various types and from diverse sources, but largely concerning southwestern Ontario, were accessioned. The collection has grown to 8,000 linear feet and includes three major categories of records: municipal records, personal manuscripts, and cartographic materials.

As the primary focus of historical studies shifted from national issues to regional, subregional and local studies during the 1960s, increased interest was directed to the holdings of the Regional Collection by faculty of the university and by other scholars. This interest led the University Library System, in collaboration with the Faculty of Social Science, to apply for and receive a University Academic Development Fund grant in 1974 to conduct a three-year project to catalog and index, in machine-readable form, the holdings of the Regional Collection.[76] The project, completed in 1977, produced a three-volume *Catalogue* and a comprehensive in-house subject index to all materials included in the *Catalogue*.[77]

The Library chose to use CODOC because it was available and seemed to meet the needs of the project. Program modifications were necessary. Additional variable-length fields with a 720-character maximum were included, and the maximum record length was increased to 2,400 characters.

[74]Carolynne Presser, "CODOC: A Computer-Based Processing and Retrieval System for Government Documents," *College and Research Libraries* 39 (March 1978): 94-98.

[75]Peter I. Hajnal, Valentina de Bruin, and Dale Biteen, "MARC and CODOC: A Case Study in Dual Format Use in a University Library," *Journal of Library Automation* 10 (December 1977): 358-373.

[76]The use of the term, "catalog," in the description of this application and in others, is problematic. As is evident from the illustration, the entries in the Personal Manuscripts *Catalogue* are quite similar to those appearing in the *Guide to the Smithsonian Archives;* and the Municipal Records *Catalogue* is essentially an alphabetical and hierarchical listing of record series. These distinctions will increasingly become unimportant with the adoption of automated systems which can produce the same information in a variety of formats, or systems which can produce the same information on-line. Of far greater concern is the adoption of standard descriptive elements to be included in all bibliographic records for archives and manuscripts.

[77]Stephanie L. Sykes, ed., *Regional Collection, The D.B. Weldon Library Catalogue* (London, Ont.: University of Western Ontario, 1977).

CORPORATE AUTHOR CATALOGUE - MUNICIPAL MANUSCRIPTS

PAGE 172

HURON COUNTY, ONT. COURT OF QUEEN'S BENCH COMMON PLEAS
PROCEDURE BOOK OF THE COURT OF QUEEN'S BENCH -- COMMON
PLEAS, HURON COUNTY, 1881-1890.
CA3ON-HU 750-Y1-P61 - F-E

HURON COUNTY, ONT. CROWN ATTORNEY
CORRESPONDENCE AND MISCELLANEOUS PAPERS OF THE HURON
COUNTY CROWN ATTORNEY, 1859, 1860, 1865-1875.
CA3ON-HU 300-V9-C55 - C-E

HURON COUNTY, ONT. DIVISION COURT
CASES OF THE HURON COUNTY DIVISION COURT, 1840, 1842-1844,
1847, 1848, 1850-1897, 1899, 1900, 1907, 1908.
CA3ON-HU 450-U0-C13 - O-E

EXECUTION BOOK FOR THE HURON COUNTY DIVISION COURT, 1856.
CA3ON-HU 450-V6-E91 - O-E

MINUTES OF THE SEVENTH DIVISION COURT, HURON COUNTY, 1856-
1864.
CA3ON-HU 450-V6-J711 - C-E

RECORD BOOK OF THE HURON COUNTY DIVISION COURT, 1860-1894.
CA3ON-HU 450-W0-R21 - C-E

HURON COUNTY, ONT. HIGH COURT OF JUSTICE
CASES OF THE HIGH COURT OF JUSTICE, HURON COUNTY, 1896-
1920.
CA3ON-HU 925-Z6-C13 - O-E

HURON COUNTY, ONT. HOUSE OF REFUGE COMMITTEE
ACCOUNTS OF THE HURON COUNTY HOUSE OF REFUGE COMMITTEE,
1919-1921.
CA3ON-HU I82-19-A13 - O-E

PROCEEDINGS OF THE HOUSE OF REFUGE COMMITTEE, HURON COUNTY,
1903-1917.
CA3ON-HU I82-03-P63 - O-E

Figure 13. Corporate Author Catalogue. (Reprinted, by permission, from Stephanie L. Sykes, ed., *Regional Collection, The D.B. Weldon Library Catalogue,* vol. I, *Municipal Records.* London, Ont.: University of Western Ontario, 1977, p. 172.)

```
        AUTHOR CATALOGUE - PERSONAL MANUSCRIPTS

                        PAGE   28


CAMERON, DONALD MACKENZIE, 1843-1936
    PAPERS OF DONALD MACKENZIE CAMERON, MERCHANT AND SHERIFF
    OF STRATHROY, 1869-1905.
        CAMERON WAS SHERIFF OF MIDDLESEX COUNTY FROM 1894 TO
        1921. EARLIER HE WAS ASSOCIATED WITH THE BUSINESS,
        CAMERON & SON (WM. & DONALD M.), EST. 1880,
        STRATHROY. RECORDS INCLUDE: FAMILY LETTERS,
        ADMINISTRATIVE RECORDS, 1893-1900, LEDGER AND
        ACCOUNTS OF CAMERON & SON, 1869-1895, SAMUEL CARROLL
        PAPERS, STRATHROY, AND GRAND TRUNK RAILWAY PAPERS
        1887-1899.
                            CA9ON-CAM011-W9-P12    - O-E


CAMERON, EMMA, D. 1917
    PAPERS OF EMMA CAMERON, WIDOW OF A. D. CAMERON, COAL
    MERCHANT OF LONDON, 1848-1905.
        PAPERS INCLUDE DEEDS FOR THE SITE OF COAL BUSINESS - A.
        D. CAMERON & SON, 316 BURWELL ST., LONDON,
        AGREEMENTS UNDATED, 1855 - 1889 BETWEEN A. D.
        CAMERON AND GEORGE D. CAMERON AND EMMA CAMERON. ALSO
        ADMINISTRATIVE RECORDS 1848 - 1905 AND GENERAL
        ACCOUNTS 1857 - 1889. AFTER A. D. CAMERON'S DEATH,
        EMMA TRANSFERRED HER INTEREST IN THE CAMERON
        BUSINESS TO HER SON, GEORGE, IN 1889.
                            CA9ON-CAM012-U8-P12    - O-E


CAMERON, MALCOLM GRAEME, 1857-1925
    LETTERS AND ACCOUNT BOOK OF MALCOLM GRAEME CAMERON,
    BARRISTER, GODERICH, 1905-1914.
        CAMERON WAS A PARTNER IN THE FIRM OF CAMERON AND
        KILLORAN. MATERIAL INCLUDES LETTERS RECEIVED, 1905,
        1906, 1910-1914. LETTERS 1910, 1911 ARE MAINLY
        POLITICAL WHILE THOSE FROM 1913, 1914 RELATE TO
        LEGAL AFFAIRS. INCLUDED ALSO IS J. L. KILLORAN'S
        ACCOUNT BOOK, SEAFORTH, 1906-1912 AND A
        MISCELLANEOUS CASE REGISTER.
                            CA9ON-CAM122-05-L21    - O-E
```

Figure 14. Author Catalogue. (Reprinted, by permission, from Stephanie L. Sykes, ed., *Regional Collection, The D.B. Weldon Library Catalogue,* vol. III, *Personal Manuscripts.* London, Ont.: University of Western Ontario, 1977, p. 28.)

The listing of record series in the municipal records volumes of the *Catalogue* is hierarchical by geographic and governmental divisions. Also included within the appropriate geographic divisions are the maps pertaining to that area. Preceding this listing of series is a corporate author index to the jurisdictional subdivisions contained within the *Catalogue*. In the personal manuscripts volume of the *Catalogue* the collections are listed alphabetically along with scope and content information. The collection descriptions are preceded by an "author index." This catalog describes the records of voluntary and commercial organizations as well as those of private individuals and families.

The *Catalogue* was produced by photoreproduction of unlined 8-½-by-11-inch line printer output. In addition to the printed catalog, a COM version was produced. The KWOC subject index was generated from series and collection titles, but additional indexing terms were frequently added. Two persons carried out most of the work, and the total cost, including the printing of the *Catalogue*, was approximately $60,000. The project was run on IBM equipment using punched card input.

CODOC programs are available through a leasing agreement.[78] While the versatility of this system is limited by its small record size, it may prove attractive to those state archives which also have responsibility for state government publications.

Corning Glass Works Archives Photonegative Computer Index

The system used by the Corning Glass Works Archives to produce indexes to photographic negatives was created for a single application. The Corning Archives holds a collection of approximately 150,000 negatives dating from 1851 which document the operation of the Corning Glass Works and life in and around Corning, New York. The collection has considerable documentary value and is also quite useful for public relations activities. A project was initiated to identify and list the negatives, to improve their physical storage, and to provide specific personal name, topic, and chronological access. In cooperation with the corporate archivist, the Corning computer services division, by combining standard IBM utility programs with new programs and interface routines, created a software package to meet the specific requirements of this project.

The system runs on IBM equipment, with punched card input, operates in a batch processing mode, and has a maximum record length of 160 characters. The record includes three fields: an accession number field, a date field, and a subject indexing field. From these records the system generates a list arranged by accession number, a keyword subject index, and selective chronological lists, either by specific year or a span of years. The keyword index is similar to a KWOC index. A string of indexing terms is entered into the field, and index entries are generated from the first word in the field and from any subsequent word which the indexer designates by placing a hyphen before the term. The other terms in the indexing string appear with each index entry. The indexing terms and their order of entry are drawn from a "category list" specifically designed for the project. While quite effective for this project, the system lacks both the versatility and some of the refinements in output formats which archivists and users appreciate in computer-generated finding aids.

ARCHON

Of the computer systems examined to this point, none have been designed to provide the user with the capacity to search the archival data base interactively. The ARCHON system, designed and used by the Baltimore Region Institutional Studies Center (BRISC), does have interactive search capabilities, as well as the capacity to produce printed indexes. The system provides comprehensive folder-level access to BRISC holdings which document the functions of Baltimore metropolitan institutions.

Since 1970, BRISC, a department of the University of Baltimore, has collected records of governmental, religious, private, and community organizations. As of the fall of 1978, its holdings included twenty-six record groups (3,500 cu.ft.), ranging from the papers of Maryland Governor Theodore R. McKeldin to the records of the Baltimore City Department of Planning, the Maryland Council of Churches, and Planned Parenthood.[79] BRISC seeks to provide users with precise folder-level access to documents relevant to traditional kinds of urban research and to political/administration decision-making processes.[80] Primary access is by subject, geographic location, and date.[81] BRISC uses computer assistance to link the collections conceptually without disturbing their original order. Intellectual con-

[78]For additional information, contact Ralph Stierwalt, Office of Library Coordination, Council of Ontario Universities, Su 8039, 130 St. George Street, Toronto, Ontario, Canada M5S 2T4.

[79]Brochure titled "A Guide to the Research Facilities" (Baltimore: University of Baltimore, Baltimore Region Institutional Studies Center, 1978).

[80]Major users include academic researchers, agency or association personnel searching for information within their own records, and private citizens seeking information for their own purposes.

[81]In providing chronological access, BRISC staff deviated from conventional archival practice by indexing the date span to which the folder contents pertain, rather than the span during which the documents were created.

trol provides common patterns of access between the records of the various agencies and associations.[82]

In order to ensure consistency of description and to facilitate searching, an *Urban Information Thesaurus*[83] has been compiled. This thesaurus, developed for the BRISC program, is designed for use by indexers assigning descriptors to the content of each folder and for use by researchers devising search strategies. To assist this process, the descriptors are listed in three separate indexes, a KWOC index, an alphabetical index, and a hierarchical listing of descriptors. The KWOC index uses every word in a descriptor as a keyword. Since keywords are arranged alphabetically, all of the descriptors with a common keyword are brought together. Included in the KWOC index are "use" references leading from terms that are not accepted descriptors to preferred terms in the indexing vocabulary. The primary thesaurus index is the alphabetical index. For some terms the alphabetical index includes scope notes defining a descriptor's use in the vocabulary. This index also shows term relationships by identifying preferred terms, broader terms, narrower terms, and related terms. In the hierarchical index all descriptors are arranged in five major classes: physical environment; development and infrastructure; social environment; public affairs; and social institutions. Thus each descriptor can be seen in its contextual position in the vocabulary.[84]

Normally four to five descriptors are assigned to each folder. Geographic and chronological descriptors are used, and personal names may be included if an individual is the subject of the folder content. Specificity of subject descriptors can be increased by adding qualifiers. These qualifiers modify the descriptors by showing physical format, mode of treatment, aspect, or viewpoint from which treated, or activities and processes. Through this thesaurus, BRISC provides a sharply defined vocabulary for the indexer and allows selective searches to be tailored to the needs of individual researchers. The ARCHON system is primarily programmed in FORTRAN and was designed for operation on an IBM 370 series computer.

Mass Transit
HX6000
SN *Refers to public transit characterized by prescribed routes and schedules along a gvien right way [Abrams]. Use 'Rapid Transit' when the right of way is exclusively reserved to a 'Mass Transit' system (e.g. 'Subways').*
BT Public Transit
NT Rapid Transit
RT Buses
Passenger Transportation
Streetcars
Subways
Transportation Networks

Master Plans
TS2109
SN *Refers to long range plans intended to guide the growth and development of an area. May include capital improvement and community development programs.*
UF Comprehensive Plans
BT Plans
RT Capital Improvement Programs
Conceptual Plans

Materials Handling
WW2707
BT Industrial Management

Maternal Care
Use: Obstetrical Care

Mathematics
MP3802
BT Physical Sciences
NT Statistics
RT Biology
Logic

Mayors
WH2902
UF City Managers
BT Municipal Government
RT Administrators and Managers
City Councils
City Halls
Elected Officials

Figure 15. Alphabetical Main Index. (Reprinted, by permission, from W.T. Dürr and Paul M. Rosenberg, *The Urban Information Thesaurus.* Westport, Ct.: Greenwood Press, 1977, p. 209. Prepared at the University of Baltimore by the Baltimore Region Institutional Studies Center.)

System Developed for the Survey of Sources for the History of Biochemistry and Molecular Biology

A multi-purpose, interactive system has been developed recently for the Survey of Sources for the History of Biochemistry and Molecular Biology conducted by the American Academy of Arts and Sciences. When, in 1976, the project director evaluated available automated systems, he found none to be appropriate for use by his project. Neither the few existing archival systems nor more sophisticated information retrieval systems were adequate for meeting the following system structure criteria:

[82] Adele N. Newburger and Paul M. Rosenberg, "Automation and Access: Finding Aids for Urban Archives," *Drexel Library Quarterly* 13, 49-51.

[83] W.T. Dürr and Paul M. Rosenberg, *The Urban Information Thesaurus: A Vocabulary for Social Documentation* (Westport, Ct.; Greenwood Press, 1976).

[84] *Ibid.*, xix-xxiii.

(1)   More than one distinctly structured data base can be constructed.

(2)   Data bases can be linked for search or index purposes, or used separately.

(3)   System does not contain restrictive limits on length or number of data fields.

(4)   System can function with missing data in any variable.

(5)   System does not contain restrictive limits on length or number of records.

(6)   Records may be subdivided as desired.

(7)   Any data element may be searched.

(8)   Indexes can be generated on any term.

(9)   System can accommodate multi-level index terms.

(10) Data bases can be searched by Boolean operators.[85]

The available archival systems did not have the sophisticated search and data base manipulation capabilities desired. Other information retrieval systems examined did not have the large, variable record lengths nor numerous large, variable-length and variable-occurrence fields necessary for effective archival description. As a result of this investigation, it was determined that new software should be created.

Software development was completed in 1978, and the resulting archival information retrieval system largely satisfies all of the stated criteria. The archival data base can be searched by Boolean operators, on-line or off-line. Data is input by punched cards, and output is available at a terminal, by line printer or on computer output microfiche. The system has also been used to create a data base containing biographical information on scientists and a bibliographic data base containing fully indexed secondary source citations relevant to the history of biochemistry and molecular biology. The software is programmed in PL/1 and designed for operation on a large IBM computer. The total cost of software development was approximately $20,000. The Survey of Sources was finished in the summer of 1979, and the software and complete system documentation is available for the cost of copying.

The system docs have limitations. For example, output formats are set to project specifications and variations of them would require reprogramming. Also, maintenance of an expanding data base could prove expensive. However, the most important consideration is that the system will not be supported; maintenance and development are the responsibility of users.[86]

PARADIGM

PARADIGM was developed at the University of Illinois at Urbana-Champaign for the university archives and has been in use there since 1971. Initially, the system was implemented to reduce the amount of clerical work needed to maintain administrative control of the archives holdings and to facilitate the tabulation, calculation, and printing of its annual report. Originally, an 80-column card was created for each of the 2,560 record series in the archives, and information concerning each series was recorded. This information included series numbers, type and status of material, volume, inclusive dates, acquisition and processing dates, length of finding aids, short series title, and subject coding. Subject coding was severely limited by the short record length, and, until 1974, the system was used primarily for collection management purposes.

Although the administrative use of PARADIGM has continued, since 1974 the system has been used increasingly to provide subject access at the series level. In that year subject indexing information was converted to a separate data base. This expanded subject coding capabilities somewhat, but since 1977, with the introduction of on-line data entry and editing capabilities,[87] any number of subject descriptors can be assigned to each series. However, it is still necessary to enter the data in 80-column segments.

Approximately 900 series in the university archives are now subject indexed; subject indexing is not necessary for the other 2,300 series, mainly publications, because their title and provenance indicate subject content. To index a series, an archivist examines the series description recorded on 5-by-8-inch Kardex cards and supplementary finding aids, selects subject descriptors from an authority list of about 2,600 descriptors, and assigns six-digit numerical codes for each descriptor. From this a series-level subject index can be printed. A conceptual approach has been adopted in the indexing of the archives, and personal name indexing is not included. The system has not been used to provide access at the box, folder, or document level.

[85]David Bearman, "Automated Access to Archival Information: Assessing Systems," *American Archivist* 42, 186.

[86]*Ibid.,* 187-189.

[87]It is important to note that this capacity for on-line terminal access to PARADIGM data bases is provided by system software of the University of Illinois IBM 360 facility rather than by programs of the PARADIGM software. In a similar fashion, the Cornell Department of Manuscripts and University Archives has developed its own SPINDEX data entry program which allows data entry at an on-line terminal. However, the most significant benefit of the new program is that it allows the Cornell archives to use the sophisticated data entry and editing capabilities of CMS (Conversational Monitor System), an interactive operating system of the IBM 370/168 computer system at Cornell. In evaluating software packages, it is important to know which system capabilities result from local system software. This does not mean that the same or similar capabilities cannot be utilized at another computer facility, but it will require investigation.

RECORD GROUP	OFFICE RECORDS	PAPERS	PUBLICATIONS	TOTAL PROCESSED
00-GENERAL	0 - .0	0 - .0	10 - 9.7	10 - 9.7
01-TRUSTEES	17 - 61.8	6 - 11.9	5 - 10.9	28 - 84.6
02-PRESIDENT	91 - 704.7	21 - 74.1	37 - 15.6	149 - 794.4
03-COUNCIL	4 - 3.7	0 - .0	0 - .0	4 - 3.7
04-SENATE	30 - 94.2	0 - .0	46 - 9.1	76 - 103.3
05-ACADEMIC DEVELOPMENT	13 - 52.5	3 - 19.6	15 - 3.8	31 - 75.9
06-PLANNING AND ALLOCATION	14 - 156.0	0 - .0	20 - 7.1	34 - 163.1
07-GRADUATE	11 - 38.6	3 - 2.2	45 - 40.6	59 - 81.4
08-AGRICULTURE	77 - 409.9	41 - 81.0	320 - 114.1	438 - 605.0
09-COMMERCE	11 - 112.1	25 - 167.7	76 - 17.2	112 - 297.0
10-EDUCATION	18 - 81.3	17 - 55.0	85 - 21.7	120 - 158.0
11-ENGINEERING	30 - 75.4	42 - 117.4	153 - 56.8	225 - 249.6
12-FINE ARTS	21 - 58.0	18 - 39.6	72 - 17.9	111 - 115.5
13-JOURNALISM	14 - 113.5	3 - 5.3	35 - 4.9	52 - 123.7
14-LAW	0 - .0	8 - 22.1	15 - 7.8	23 - 29.9
15-LIBERAL ARTS	64 - 282.9	104 - 419.3	154 - 34.9	322 - 737.1
16-PHYSICAL EDUCATION	4 - 10.9	6 - 5.3	36 - 3.8	46 - 20.0
17-VETERINARY MEDICINE	2 - 21.6	1 - .3	21 - 2.8	24 - 24.7
18-LIBRARY SCIENCE	34 - 106.3	5 - 23.6	32 - 9.3	71 - 139.2
19-SOCIAL WORK	1 - 6.3	0 - .0	4 - .4	5 - 6.7
20-AVIATION, INSTITUTE OF	3 - 10.2	1 - 1.3	10 - 1.2	14 - 12.7
21-GOVT AND PUBLIC AFFAIRS	1 - 12.0	0 - .0	13 - 2.2	14 - 14.2
22-LABOR AND IND RELATIONS	1 - 13.6	2 - 2.9	16 - 4.8	19 - 21.3
23-ENVIRONMENTAL STUDIES	0 - .0	0 - .0	4 - 2.7	4 - 2.7
24-CHANCELLOR	10 - 18.6	0 - .0	19 - 4.0	29 - 22.6
25-ADMISSIONS AND RECORDS	19 - 354.7	1 - 2.3	34 - 15.9	54 - 372.9
26-ALUMNI	17 - 148.3	56 - 343.4	24 - 10.2	97 - 501.9
27-ARMED FORCES	6 - 2.7	1 - .1	11 - 1.6	18 - 4.4
28-ATHLETIC ASSOCIATION	9 - 3.7	3 - 3.2	18 - 9.4	30 - 16.3
29-CIVIL SERVICE	0 - .0	0 - .0	5 - 1.2	5 - 1.2
30-DADS AND MOTHERS	1 - .3	0 - .0	7 - 2.8	8 - 3.1
31-CONTINUING EDUCATION	1 - 1.0	2 - .2	61 - 12.1	64 - 13.3
32-FOUNDATION	3 - 11.7	1 - 2.4	13 - 1.6	17 - 15.7
33-HEALTH SERVICE	0 - .0	0 - .0	9 - 2.8	9 - 2.8
34-LEGAL COUNSEL	1 - 35.7	0 - .0	0 - .0	1 - 35.7
35-LIBRARY	38 - 110.1	14 - 15.8	22 - 5.4	74 - 131.3
36-NONACADEMIC PERSONNEL	1 - 8.0	0 - .0	13 - 1.5	14 - 9.5
37-PHYSICAL PLANT	13 - 47.1	0 - .0	35 - 7.1	48 - 54.2
38-PRESS	1 - .3	1 - 11.6	12 - 51.3	14 - 63.2
39-PUBLIC INFORMATION	14 - 94.3	3 - 59.1	6 - 2.9	23 - 156.3
40-RETIREMENT	0 - .0	0 - .0	8 - .8	8 - .8
41-STUDENT AFFAIRS	38 - 823.0	100 - 78.4	97 - 99.6	235 - 1001.0
43-NATURAL HISTORY	14 - 29.3	5 - 8.1	17 - 6.1	36 - 43.5
44-GEOLOGICAL SURVEY	0 - .0	0 - .0	14 - 7.9	14 - 7.9
45-WATER SURVEY	1 - .1	0 - .0	11 - 4.7	12 - 4.8
48-FACULTY	5 - 1.5	10 - 20.2	1 - 53.0	16 - 74.7
49-GALESBURG	1 - 3.0	0 - .0	12 - 1.3	13 - 4.3
50-59-MEDICAL CENTER	8 - 1.4	3 - 4.8	102 - 18.6	113 - 24.8
60-67-CHICAGO CIRCLE	1 - .3	0 - .0	51 - 9.0	52 - 9.3
TOTAL	663 - 4120.6	506 - 1598.2	1826 - 730.1	2995 - 6448.9

Figure 16. Table 2 of the "Twelfth Annual Report of the University of Illinois University Archives, July 1, 1974 - June 30, 1975." (Urbana, Ill., 1975, p. 15-16. Reprinted by permission of the author, Maynard J. Brichford.)

RECORDS OF THE GOVERNMENT OF THE DISTRICT OF COLUMBIA   8   Date of this inventory: 25 FEB 1977.

vote of the council. In addition, Congress has retained veto power over local actions, as well as many other local legislative and regulatory powers. Congress also has continued annual Federal payments to the District to compensate for local taxes not paid by the tax-exempt Federal establishment.

An act of September 22, 1970 (84 Stat. 848) has allowed the citizens of the District to elect a nonvoting delegate to the House of Representatives who serves for the duration of each Congress.

```
                          1660
                          1670
                          1680
                          1690
                          1700
                          1710
                          1720
                          1730
```

General Records

`0000-0000  NNFN  351  1  1`

RECORDS OF THE OFFICE OF MAYOR

`0000-0000  NNFN  351  1  1  1`
`            NNFN  351  1  1  1   1`

1. MANUSCRIPT LAWS OF THE CITY OF WASHINGTON.   1 vol.
    1838-1839.   4 cm, 1 in.

    Arranged in two parts as described below.
    The first part of the volume, which is arranged chronologically and numbered 1-95, consists of official copies of private and public acts and resolutions passed by the corporation from July 5, 1838 through May 31, 1839. The ordinances are signed by the president of the Board of Common Council, the President of the Board of Aldermen; and the Mayor, Peter Force. The last part of the volume, which is arranged chronologically, consists of petitions, bills for services rendered, written opinions of city officials, and other miscellaneous documents.

```
Line
10
20
30
40
50
60
70
80
90
```

`NNFN  351  1  1   2`

2. LETTERS SENT.   1 vol.
    Oct. 19, 1857-Oct. 19, 1863.   6 cm, 2 in.

    Arranged chronologically.
    Handwritten copies of official letters sent by Mayors William B. Magruder, James G. Barret, and Richard Wallach. Most of the letters are addressed to the Board of Common Council or the Board of Aldermen, informing them of official actions taken by the Mayor, including bills signed, personal actions, recommendations, responses to resolutions, and similar subjects. There are also a few letters of appointment and several letters to city officials concerning their duties.

```
Line
10
20
30
40
50
60
70
80
```

`NNFN  351  1  1  1   3`

3. JOURNAL OF RECEIPTS.   1 vol.
    Feb. 19, 1858-Dec. 13, 1859.   5 cm, 2 in.

    Arranged chronologically and thereunder by name of account.
    Entries give date, number and name of account credited (general fund, sinking fund, school fund, etc.), name of payee, and amount received.

```
Line
10
20
30
```

`0000-0000  NNFN  351  1  1   2`
`            NNFN  351  1  1  2   1`

RECORDS OF THE TERRITORIAL GOVERNMENT

4. LAWS OF THE LEGISLATIVE ASSEMBLY.   2 vols.
    Jun. 2, 1871-Jun. 20, 1874.   1 cm, 1/2 in.

    Arranged chronologically.
    Official copies of public and private acts and resolutions of the Assembly relating to all aspects of local government, including appointments, appropriations, assessments, health regulations, relief of the poor, local election, public works, business regulations, public works.

```
Line
10
20
30
40
50
```

Figure 17. A page from the preliminary edition of the "Preliminary Inventory of the Records of the Government of the District of Columbia (Record Group 351)." (Dorothy S. Provine, comp. Washington, D.C.: National Archives and Records Service, General Services Administration, 1977, p. 8)

Since 1976, PARADIGM has also been used to provide similar administrative control and subject indexing for 400 series of the American Library Association (ALA) archives, which are maintained at the University of Illinois. A different subject authority list is used, and the names of persons, associations, divisions, and committees are also included. PARADIGM is also being used in the creation of a National Catalog of Sources for the History of Librarianship (NCSHL). On-line access is provided to coded information regarding manuscript collections relating to librarianship in other repositories, and printed subject indexes are being generated.[88] PARADIGM is programmed in COBOL and is run on an IBM 360 series computer.

NARS A-1

The development of the NARS A-1 system is a response by NARS to the need to establish comprehensive administrative control of its holdings. To accomplish this goal, NARS A-1 has been designed to: (1) provide effective administrative control over all record groups through the production of a variety of management and statistical reports; and (2) provide comprehensive series-level description by compiling all series descriptions into one machine-readable master file. The system was designed during 1974-75, and implementation began in 1976.

NARS A-1 is considered to be a computer-assisted rather than a computer-centered system. It is a text editing, or word processing, system. EDP capabilities are used to enhance a largely clerical process rather than to retrieve information. The information entered and maintained by the system differs little from that maintained manually in the past, and the primary output products are designed to resemble traditional NARS inventory and reporting formats. The primary benefits of this system are in the areas of more efficient storage, revision, updating and reporting of information. And these are accomplishments for a repository as large as the National Archives. While the nature of the objectives is modest, the size of the task is huge.

The primary mode of system operation is batch processing. Files are sequentially arranged according to a hierarchical numbering scheme which reflects the originating agency's organizational and/or functional structure. Records and fields are fixed-length, but the use of set identification codes allows the entry of text narratives of extensive length.

To avoid limitations resulting from total dependence on the General Services Administration

(GSA) for computer services, the National Archives purchased a minicomputer (Four Phase, Data IV/90). Data input and a small statistical file can be handled on-line with COBOL software provided with the minicomputer. The input program includes simultaneous data entry and background processing abilities, data validation and various automatic editing features, and format control. Batch processing of entire files is done at the GSA computer facilities and the master file is stored there on magnetic tape. NARS estimates that the A-1 data base will grow to about 100 million characters over the next twenty years (estimated period for project completion). This growth will require some revision of the current sequential tape system. However, further development of the minicomputer system eventually may provide on-line, control-number access to series descriptions.

After three years experience, NARS estimates an average production rate of 6,000 series descriptions per year with four input operators. Total annual costs (with start-up costs distributed over a period of twenty years) are estimated to be $74,350 per year or $12.39 per series.[89]

There are several other automated systems presently being used by archivists in the United State and Canada, but this survey should provide a realistic sense of the current state of the art. Archivists who adopt automated techniques during the 1980s can benefit from and improve on the experiences of those who began in the 1970s.

---

[89]Alan Calmes, "Practical Realities of Computer-based Finding Aids: The NARS A-1 Experience," *American Archivist* 42, 167-177.

Suggested Readings

Aitchison, Jean, and Gilchrist, Alan. *Thesaurus Construction: A Practical Manual.* London: Aslib, 1972.

Austin, Derek, and Digger, Jeremy A. "PRECIS: the Preserved Context Index System." *Library Resources and Technical Services* 21 (Winter 1977): 13-30.

Bain, Alan L. "Computer Applications to Archives and Manuscripts at the Smithsonian Institution Archives." *ADPA* 2 (August 1978): 13-21.

Bell, Lionel. "Controlled Vocabulary Indexing of Archives." *Journal of the Society of Archivists* 4 (October 1971): 285-299.

Bell, Lionel. "Survey of Archival Data Processing." *ADPA* 1 (August 1975): 11-26.

---

[88]"PARADIGM Automated Data Processing System," (Urbana, Illinois: University Archives, University of Illinois at Urbana-Champaign, 1978), 1-2.

Calmes, Alan. "Practical Realities of Computer-based Finding Aids: The NARS A-1 Experience." *American Archivist* 42 (April 1979): 167-177.

Hannestad, Stephen E. "SPINDEX II: A Computerized Approach to Preparing Guides to Archives and Manuscripts." *Computing in the Humanities: Proceedings of the 3rd International Conference on Computing in the Humanities,* ed. Serge Lusignan and John S. North. Waterloo, Ont.: University of Waterloo Press, 1977.

Hickerson, H. Thomas, ed. *SPINDEX Users Conference: Proceedings of a Meeting Held at Cornell University, Ithaca, New York, March 31 and April 1, 1978.* Ithaca, N.Y.: Department of Manuscripts and University Archives, Cornell University Libraries, 1979.

Hickerson, H. Thomas; Winters, Joan; and Beale, Venetia. *SPINDEX II at Cornell University and a Review of Archival Automation in the United States.* Ithaca, N.Y.: Department of Manuscripts and University Archives, Cornell University Libraries, 1976.

Lancaster, F. Wilfrid, and Owen, Jeanne M. "Information Retrieval by Computer." *The Information Age: Its Development, Its Impact,* ed. Donald P. Hammer. Metuchen, N.J.: The Scarecrow Press, Inc., 1976.

Lytle, Richard H. "Intellectual Access to Archives: I. Provenance and Content Indexing Methods of Subject Retrieval." *American Archivist* 43 (Winter 1980): 64-75.

Lytle, Richard H. "Intellectual Access to Archives: II Report of an Experiment Comparing Provenance and Content Indexing Methods of Subject Retrieval." *American Archivist* 43 (Spring 1980): 191-207.

Newberger, Adele M., and Rosenberg, Paul M. "Automation and Access: Finding Aids for Urban Archives." *Drexel Library Quarterly* 13 (October 1977): 45-59.

Salton, Gerard, and Wong, Anita. "On the Role of Words and Phrases in Automatic Text Analysis." *Computers and the Humanities* 10 (March/April 1976): 69-87.

Soergel, Dagobert. *Indexing Languages and Thesauri: Construction and Maintenance.* Los Angeles: Melville Publishing Company, 1974.

Torchia, Marion M. "Two Experiments in Automated Indexing: The Presidential Papers and the Papers of the Continental Congress." *American Archivist* 39 (October 1976): 437-445.

4 Implementing Automated Techniques

Archivists perform a broad variety of information processing functions. They devise and implement acquisition policies. They evaluate offers of records and papers to determine which documents should be preserved and which ones discarded. Retained records are accessioned. Information concerning provenance is recorded. Temporary locations are assigned, and processing priorities and conservation steps are determined. Arrangement and description procedures are specified. Information concerning the records may be included in a card catalog, a record group or series inventory, or a cumulative index to repository holdings. Some or all of this information may be submitted to a national guide and selected journals. Reference statistics are compiled. To facilitate use, a more detailed finding aid may be created and published, an exhibit may be organized, or a microfilm edition of the records may be produced. These basic functions are common to most repositories; it is thus evident that even a small archival operation can be a complex system.[90]

Computers could assist in all of these archival processes and in other administrative functions. The preceding chapter surveyed the efforts of some archivists to use EDP. Most frequently, automation is being used to improve intellectual access to archival holdings. In addition computers are being used to manage information and to facilitate the reproduction of descriptive data by COM and electronic photocomposition. The range of potential uses is extensive. However, the design of any computer application should be preceded by a careful examination of existing methods of operation. Therefore, this chapter begins by describing methods of analyzing current practices and articulating realistic objectives. The chapter then examines steps in the design and implementation of automated processes. The chapter concludes with a discussion of professional cooperation in the development and use of automated techniques.

Careful examination and evaluation of existing methods of operation is a prerequisite to automation. If this examination is carried out in a systematic fashion, it

---

[90]The term "system" is used here to describe an assemblage of interrelated parts, including methods, equipment, funding, information, and personnel, united into a coherent whole and possessing a common goal or objective. The following references to archival systems concern integrated processes, either manual or automated, carried out in the operation of an archival repository, rather than specific computer software packages or computer hardware configurations.

can provide valuable insights concerning both practices and objectives. Specifically, archivists may find that certain procedures create ambiguity and confusion because they conflict with, rather than complement, other repository procedures. Certain types of finding aids, which are produced routinely, may be of little value to staff or users; and processes may be continuing, the objectives of which have been rejected long ago. Also, this examination should prevent the adoption of new methods in one area while parallel processes are continued in another. Most important, such an examination should result in more clearly defined program objectives and a better understanding of those processes which aid or hinder the accomplishment of those goals. This preliminary analysis is vital, not for the discovery of what computers can do, but for learning what it is that needs to be done at a repository.[91]

An important, initial step in this process is the identification of overall system objectives. Both internal objectives (direct results or products of system processes) and external objectives (the external effects of archives' action and policies) should be considered. Each objective should be defined in terms of the expected performance of the system. Statements of expected performance assist in keeping objectives realistic and meaningful, preventing a dichotomy from developing between real and stated objectives.[92] A realistic statement of objectives can be used to determine which operations contribute effectively to the accomplishment of expressed goals and to design and evaluate new processes to meet the objectives.[93]

Having defined repository objectives, the next step is the identification and examination of the relationships among those processes which comprise the system. In seeking to develop an accurate perception of repository functions and the manner in which one process interacts with another, an effective method is the use of *flowcharts.*

Flowcharting is the graphic representation of a sequence of operations. By using a few standard symbols (see Figure 18) connected by lines (flowlines), the logical flow of an operation can be portrayed. A flowchart both identifies the steps in a process and defines their sequence. Generally, certain rules are accepted in the construction of all types of flowcharts. Normally, the direction of flow is from top to bottom or from left to right.

[91]Francis J.G. Robinson, et al., *Systems Analysis in Libraries,* Symplegades: A Series of Papers on Computers, Libraries and Information Processing, No. II (Newcastle upon Tyne, England: Oriel Press Limited, 1969): 1.

[92]Robert W. Burns, Jr., "A Generalized Methodology for Library Systems Analysis," *College and Research Libraries* 32, 300.

[93]Robinson, et al., *Systems Analysis in Libraries,* 3.

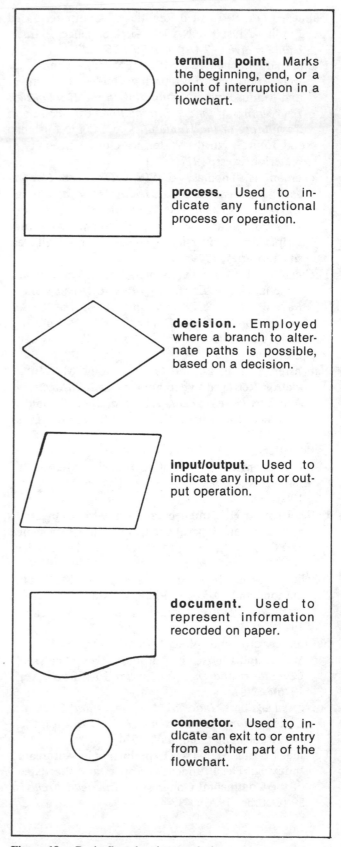

terminal point. Marks the beginning, end, or a point of interruption in a flowchart.

process. Used to indicate any functional process or operation.

decision. Employed where a branch to alternate paths is possible, based on a decision.

input/output. Used to indicate any input or output operation.

document. Used to represent information recorded on paper.

connector. Used to indicate an exit to or entry from another part of the flowchart.

Figure 18.   Basic flowcharting symbols

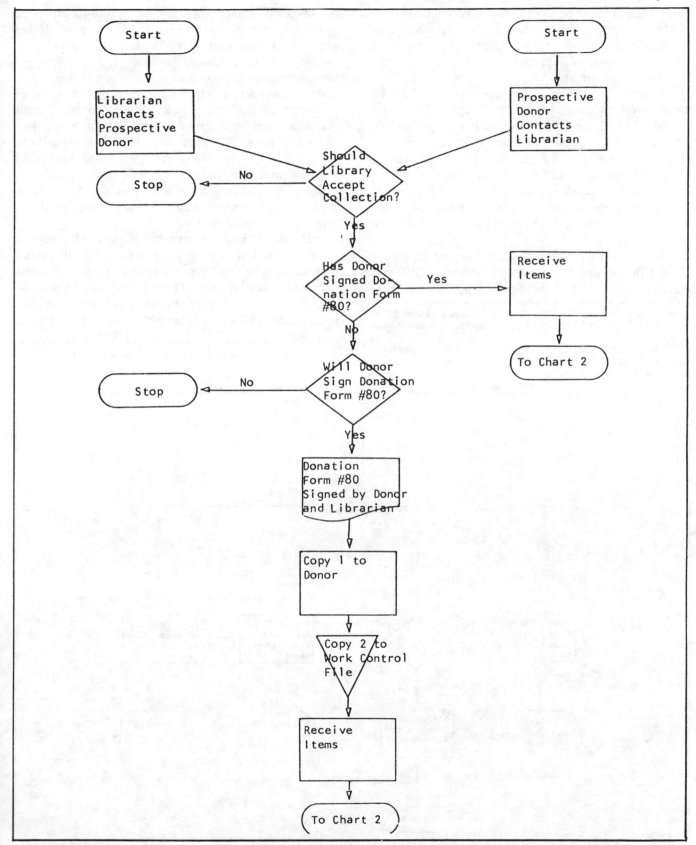

Figure 19. Flowchart #1: Acquiring a New Collection or Addition to Existing Collection. (Reprinted, by permission, from *Archives Procedural Manual*. St. Louis: Washington University School of Medicine Library, 1974, p. 7.)

Arrowheads should be used if the direction of flow is anything else.[94] Flowcharts should be kept as simple and straightforward as possible.[95] Charts that are cluttered with excessive detail lose their logical simplicity and become less informative.

Figures 19 and 20 represent processes carried out by the archival program of the Washington University School of Medicine Library. These two charts are the first of twenty-one charts included in its *Archives Procedural Manual* (St. Louis: Washington University School of Medicine Library, 1974). These charts illustrate the important connective feature of flowcharts, the output of one process is the input to another.[96] This aspect of flowcharting is important in defining the role of a particular process in the overall system.

Flowcharting is a flexible technique and can be applied with varying degrees of refinement to different parts of a system. The logical consistency of flowcharting makes it equally applicable to simple functions or to complex processes. However, it should be noted, that although a flowchart may illustrate the logical consistency of a particular procedure, it offers no assurance that the procedure is logically justified.[97] Nor does a flowchart tell whether the value of the resources necessary to perform a task is equal to the benefit resulting from its accomplishment. Careful analysis of costs and benefits is necessary. In this analysis both tangibles (wages, supplies, space, etc.) and intangibles (convenience, prestige, etc.) must be considered. Neither the continuance of a current practice nor the adoption of a new procedure should be based solely on sentiment or intuition.[98]

Having defined repository objectives and analyzed current operations, the next step is to devise automated procedures which will improve system effectiveness and support stated objectives. Theoretically, the design process should begin after the system examination has been completed, and the results have been carefully reviewed;

[94]Arrowheads add clarity to flowcharts and can be used at all times.

[95]William S. Davis and Allison McCormack, *The Information Age,* 147.

[96]Although there may be a general progression from one process to another, the output from one process may be input to a process sequentially precedent. Also, one process may provide input to or receive output from several different processes.

[97]Robinson, et al., *Systems Analysis in Libraries,* 21-22.

[98]Burns, "A Generalized Methodology for Library Systems Analysis," 300-301.

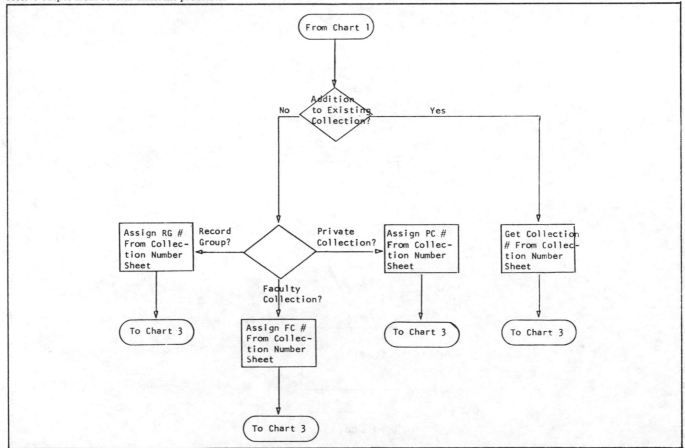

Figure 20. Flowchart #2: Assigning Collection Numbers. (Reprinted, by permission, from *Archives Procedural Manual.* St. Louis: Washington University School of Medicine Library, 1974, p. 12.)

in practice, design efforts usually start earlier. The decision to investigate the adoption of automated techniques may have been instigated by the presentation of specific automation designs. This sequence is quite natural and can be beneficial as long as initial planning does not inhibit the unbiased consideration of alternative designs. However, it must be emphasized that, before the planning phase proceeds, authorization and assurance of support must be obtained from appropriate superiors and governing boards. All too often one or two individuals design a computer application without sufficient involvement of key personnel and without adequate institutional backing. In addition, all agency staff should be notified of the planning process, and provided the opportunity to offer needed advice. Such a strategy can foster acceptance and support for system implementation.[99]

Whether the automated system being developed will serve primarily as a management information system (MIS) or as an information storage and retrieval system (ISARS) should be decided early in the planning phase. Management information systems are designed to provide information needed to understand, plan, and manage the operation of an organization. They are data retrieval systems, providing specific information upon request. In an archives, information could be produced on such matters as the volume or percentage of holdings unprocessed, monthly and annual user statistics, and the numbers of hours of staff time allocated to processing, reference service, and collection development. These retrieval systems have arithmetic and statistical capabilities, are designed to handle largely numeric data bases, and usually provide a variety of tabular reporting formats. The primary purpose of management information systems is to organize information so that it can be retrieved, when needed, for operations control and improved decision making.[100]

While archivists surely can benefit from the use of management information systems, the primary use of archival automation has been information storage and retrieval. Information storage and retrieval systems are document retrieval systems. Rather than providing specific data in response to a request for information, these systems retrieve documents or descriptions of documents that contain information relevant to the request. These are language-processing systems, capable of manipulating large files of bibliographic data. The choice between MIS and ISARS should be determined on the basis of primary objectives. This decision will affect the choice of software packages and will also influence hardware selection. Since ISARS frequently need substantial memory and storage capacity, they often require the use of large-scale computers.

After determining the general type of data processing capabilities needed, a source of computer service must be selected. Alternatives include:

(1) Using a large computer belonging to the parent institution and available on a time-sharing basis.

(2) Contracting with a service bureau for computer service. Either the bureau can provide time-sharing in the manner that institutional services are provided, or the entire data processing function can be contracted out. Recent volumes of the *National List of Manuscripts in Canadian Repositories* have been produced in this manner.

(3) Purchasing or leasing a minicomputer or microcomputer for in-house data processing. Some minicomputers have many of the capabilities of large computers and could be used to perform a broad range of archival functions. But microcomputers at this time are unacceptable alternatives for multipurpose archival use.[101]

(4) Using a minicomputer, microcomputer, or word processing device to create a machine-readable record to be processed elsewhere.

(5) Participating in a national, on-line network such as OCLC.

The source of computer service and the selection of hardware may be determined primarily by financial resources and institutional environment. The choice of software will be limited by the type of hardware available and will also be influenced by financial and institutional considerations. However, the software chosen must be compatible with the basic characteristics of archival description and provide desired access capabilities.

The services of an experienced consultant can be useful when choosing software and designing specific applications. Visiting repositories which have implemented automated techniques is also useful. In university, governmental, or corporate settings, archivists can usually obtain assistance from the staff that

[99]Robert G. Chenhall, *Museum Cataloging in the Computer Age,* 235-237.

[100]Susan Artandi, *An Introduction to Computers in Information Science,* 26-27.

[101]The versatility of microcomputers is often limited by inadequacies in available memory space and in disk storage capacity. There is no application software specifically designed for library or archival use currently available, but MARS (Microcomputer Archives and Records Management Systems), a microcomputer software system for archival use, is being developed at East Tennessee State University. "NEH Awards Two Grants to the Archives," *Archives of Appalachia Newsletter* 2 (September 1980): 1.

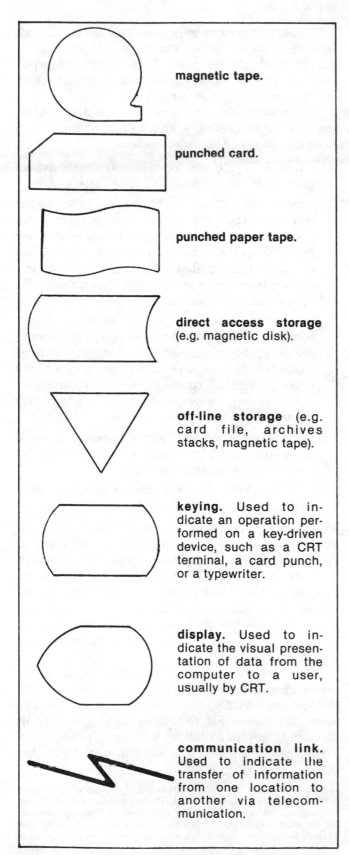

magnetic tape.

punched card.

punched paper tape.

direct access storage (e.g. magnetic disk).

off-line storage (e.g. card file, archives stacks, magnetic tape).

keying. Used to indicate an operation performed on a key-driven device, such as a CRT terminal, a card punch, or a typewriter.

display. Used to indicate the visual presentation of data from the computer to a user, usually by CRT.

communication link. Used to indicate the transfer of information from one location to another via telecommunication.

Figure 21.   Flowcharting symbols for automated processes

operates institutional computer services. When institutional time-sharing facilities are used, it is important to develop an effective working relationship with computer center personnel.

Flowcharts, using standard symbols for automated processes, should be created for newly designed archival procedures. If additional computer programming is done locally, new programs or modifications to existing software must be well documented. Equipment needs should be specified, and a selection process initiated.

For most computer applications in archives, equipment needs will be limited to I/O devices. If a line printer is purchased or leased, it must have upper/lowercase capability and must print clearly and crisply. There are two basic types of impact printers: those that use preformed characters and the dot-matrix type. Those with preformed characters strike the paper through a ribbon, like a conventional typewriter. Printers with preformed characters produce higher-quality printing than do the dot-matrix type in which characters are printed in patterns of dots, most often in a matrix of seven or nine elements. Dot-matrix printers are less expensive and somewhat faster, but, generally, they produce unattractive, or even difficult-to-read, printing.[102]

Most frequently, archivists will be required to select a CRT terminal. At present, there are hundreds of different CRT terminals available, and their purchase prices range from a few hundred to several thousand dollars. Many offer special features, such as line drawing and graphic capabilities, black-on-white or color-character display, or special data transmission modes; however, the additional costs should not be incurred if the features are not essential. If special features increase keyboard complexity, they may detract from terminal efficiency in typical use. Basic considerations include display characteristics, keyboard characteristics, character sets, speed of reception and transmission of data, and maintenance and durability. The Technical Standards for Library Automation Committee of the Information Science and Automation Section in the Library and Information Technology Association has recently developed a checklist for CRT terminals which examines these characteristics and others.[103]

In selecting I/O devices, it is useful to observe the equipment in operation. When possible, consult people who have used the equipment under consideration for purposes similar to your own. It is important to consult

---

[102]Peter S. Graham, "Terminals and Printers for Library Use: Report on a Selection," *Journal of Library Automation* 10, 350-353.

[103]Walt Crawford, "CRT Terminal Checklist," *Journal of Library Automation* 13, 36-44.

with personnel of your computer center who are familiar with local interface requirements. The choice of appropriate peripheral equipment can contribute to operating efficiency and to the production of results which are acceptable to system users.

An automated system has three principal elements: input, processing, and output. In the implementation of automated techniques and the design of specific applications, output must be considered first. The nature of the desired results will determine what input is needed. It may be that necessary input data is not easily obtained, and output demands should be reexamined.[104] Archivists must remember that while computers offer expanded capabilities for efficient processing of bibliographic data, archivists must input descriptive data of a high quality to ensure satisfactory results. It must be emphasized that a new system should not necessarily produce bibliographic aids which are exact replicas, either in appearance, content, or pattern of use, of finding aids previously produced manually. There can be a needless waste of resources in efforts to duplicate processes which, in many cases, have already been found to be inadequate. Such duplication may also severely limit the potential benefits which might be derived from the system.

After specifying the nature of desired outputs, a record format or field structure must be devised. This format is defined in terms of fields and their use. Field definitions indicate the type of information that can be recorded there, and each field is assigned an associated code or tag which clearly identifies the field (see Figure 6). Field definitions must be precise because a computer cannot make allowances for the minor discrepancies which people handle without difficulty. This descriptive format is a fundamental aspect of the system because it affects the manner in which files of information can be used.[105]

Specific formats may vary from one type of application to another, but the basic bibliographic record should be the same for all record groups or collections. The record should include necessary data for a variety of potential applications. Automation is most cost efficient when a number of different functions can be served by a single data base.

Record format not only affects the way records are entered into a data base and are processed by the computer; format also influences the manner in which documents are analyzed and described and the way the descriptive data is reported. To facilitate the descriptive process and to improve data entry efficiency, forms should be designed which can be used effectively in analysis and description and also in data entry. They should include both field titles and identifying tags. Forms should be tailored to fit specific project needs and should record all basic elements of description.

The implementation of automated techniques will increase consistency in descriptive practices within a repository. The use of EDP will also increase the adoption of standard methods of description by the various repositories of historical documentation. Archivists have sought to further the use of standard methods of description; automation significantly increases both the need for and the benefits to be derived from standarization.

The use of automation is stimulating greater cooperation among archivists and among archival institutions. Cooperation is needed because the substantial expense of developing automated systems is difficult for most institutions to bear alone. Because archival automation is a new area of knowledge and experience, archivists must share their ideas and experiences. Cooperation is also basic to the use of automation because, only through joint efforts, can archivists realize the potential that automation offers for national access to bibliographic information concerning primary source documentation.

During the decade of the 1980s, it is likely that over half of the major repositories in the United States and Canada will adopt the use of computer assistance. It is clear that archivists must direct a considerable portion of their professional resources to further the development of effective automation methods. This effort should be channeled through the Society of American Archivists (SAA), which has created a Task Force on Automated Records and Techniques and a Task Force on National Information Systems for Archives and Manuscript Collections (NIS).[106] The Automated Records and Techniques Task Force serves as a focal point for communication and coordination of activities relating to machine-readable records and archival automation and has developed an active program in the areas of education, training, and publication. The NIS Task Force was formed in 1977 to explore the possibilities for constructing a national information system for archives and manuscripts and is currently involved in efforts to establish a set of standard elements for machine-readable description of archives and

[104]Robinson, et al., *Systems Analysis in Libraries*, 44-45.
[105]Chet Gough and Taverekere Srikantaiah, *Systems Analysis in Libraries: A Question and Answer Approach*, 82-83.

[106]Richard H. Lytle, "A National Information System for Archives and Manuscript Collections," *American Archivist* 43, 423-426.

Control Number	CATALOGING WORKSHEET	Entered
		Cataloged
Call Number 400	Microform Note 600	Checked
Main Entry 120		

Title
100

Collation
900ƀƀ

Content Note
901ƀƀ

Donor Note
903ƀƀ

Donor's Name	Donation Date
700	710
Restriction Note	Opening Note
904ƀƀ	730ƀƀR:ƀƀ
Finding Aids	Anals. Note
905ƀƀ	906ƀƀ

Language	Medium	Vault
731ƀƀL:ƀƀ	732ƀƀ	740ƀƀ

Repository Note	Name Entries
733ƀ	210

Subject Entries
200

Figure 22. Cataloging Worksheet. (Reprinted with permission of the Historical Department, Church of Jesus Christ of Latter-day Saints.)

LIBRARY OF CONGRESS MANUSCRIPT DIVISION

DICTIONARY CATALOG OF COLLECTIONS ENTRY

Cataloged by:

Date Cataloged: 620

Master Record No. 001

Record Type: 008   2.#3.c   5-P

Date Revised: 620

Main Entry: 105

Form of Material: 244   Bulk Dates: 560

Items: 302#b   Units: 303   Microfilm Locator: 091#b

Series: 490   Repository: 535

General Note: 500

Scope and Content Note: 520

Finding Aid: 555

Provenance: 541

Literary Rights: 540

Restrictions: 506

1) Head, Pr. Sec.	2) Editor	3) Head, R. Ser.	4) Specialist	5) Asst. Chief	6) Chief	7) Archivist	8) Cataloger

Specialist: 037   NUCMC No. OIO   Languages: 045

Professions/Occupations: 690

C N W P R L S B H A F

References (600) Cross References (601) Added Entries (850) and other tags as necessary.

Comments:

Figure 23. Dictionary Catalog of Collections Entry. (Manuscripts Division, Library of Congress.)

manuscripts.[107] Several other groups within SAA also have initiated activities related to the use of automated systems. Contrary to this trend, however, the SAA guidelines for graduate archival education programs exclude any mention of automation or machine-readable records.[108]

There are currently two national automated systems for archives and manuscripts information. One is the NHPRC Guide Project which is using SPINDEX III to build a data base containing both descriptive information and indexing data. The Project will produce, periodically, in printed and COM form, a national guide and subject index. The record format for this project is well designed, but the sequential access requirements of a SPINDEX-generated data base limit the potential capabilities of this system.

OCLC, the other national data base for archives and manuscripts, uses the MARC II format for manuscripts and is adopting AACR II for cataloging manuscripts. In addition to this restrictive record format, subject access to records in the data base is not provided. However, OCLC does offer sophisticated, on-line access and network data transmission capabilities, as well as the production of catalog cards.

The Research Libraries Group (RLG) is also developing a national data base for archives and manuscripts, but it is not yet available, nor has a record format been designed. It will, apparently, provide online subject access. However, the ideal national system is not yet available.

In 1981, we are at an important point in the development of automated methods. The archival profession is faced with a number of significant issues which relate to the use of automation. There is now a widespread interest in facing these issues. Through SAA we should develop both the resources and the methods to do so. Archival automation may serve both as an objective and a tool in the articulation of professional goals and the development of national cooperation.

Suggested Readings

Bearman, David. "Automated Access to Archival Information: Assessing Systems." *American Archivist* 42 (April 1979): 179-190.

Bommer, M.R.; Chorba, R.W.; and Grattidge, W. "Performance Assessment Model for Academic Libraries." *Journal of the American Society for Information Science* 30 (March 1979): 93-99.

Burns, Robert W., Jr. "A Generalized Methodology for Library Systems Analysis." *College and Research Libraries* 32 (July 1971): 295-303.

Crawford, Susan, and Rees, Alan M., eds. "On-line Systems in Science and Technology." *Journal of the American Society for Information Science* 31 (May 1980): 153-200.

Crawford, Walt. "CRT Terminal Checklist." *Journal of Library Automation* 13 (March 1980): 36-44.

Darwin, Kenneth. "The Use of the Computer in Indexing Records." *Journal of the Society of Archivists* 4 (April 1971): 218-229.

Gough, Chet, and Srikantaiah, Taverekere. *Systems Analysis in Libraries: A Question and Answer Approach.* Hamden, Ct.: Linnet Books, 1978.

Graham, Peter S. "Terminals and Printers for Library Use: Report on a Selection." *Journal of Library Automation* 10 (December 1977): 343-357.

Kesner, Richard M. "The Computer's Future in Archival Management: An Evaluation." *The Midwestern Archivist* 3:2 (1978): 25-38.

Pratt, Allan D. "The Use of Microcomputers in Libraries." *Journal of Library Automation* 13 (March 1980): 7-17.

Lytle, Richard H. "A National Information System for Archives and Manuscript Collections." *American Archivist* 43 (Summer 1980): 423-426.

Markuson, Barbara Evans. "Library Networks: Progress and Problems." *The Information Age: Its Development, Its Impact,* ed. Donald P. Hammer, Metuchen, N.J.: The Scarecrow Press, Inc., 1976.

Roper, Michael. "PROSPEC—SA: A Case Study in Setting Up a Cooperative Computer Project," *ADPA* 2 (August 1977):9-14.

Wasserman, A.I. "Information System Design Methodology." *Journal of the American Society for Information Science.* 31 (January 1980): 5-24.

---

[107]Elaine D. Engst, "Standard Elements for the Description of Archives and Manuscript Collections," An unpublished report to the Society of American Archivists Task Force on National Information Systems, 1980.

[108]"Archives Education Guidelines Approved," *SAA Newsletter* (May 1977): 4-5.

Glossary*

access. The process of obtaining data from or placing data in storage.

access arm (seek arm). A movable arm which positions a read/write head so that the data can be written to or read from a magnetic disk. In a disk pack, each magnetic surface is accessed by its own individual arm. These arms move back and forth in unison between the disks.

access time. The time interval required for a computer to locate and transfer information to or from storage.

ADP. See automatic data processing.

algorithm. A prescribed set of well-defined rules or processes for solving a problem in a finite number of steps.

analog computer. A computer which processes data represented in a continuous form, as contrasted with digital computers, which process data in a discrete (discontinuous) form. Analog data are usually represented by means of physical variables, such as voltage, resistance, or rotation.

application software. Computer programs designed to perform user functions. This software operates to solve the problems of particular users, rather than to support the operation of the entire computer system.

arithmetic unit. Also known as the arithmetic and logic unit (ALU), this portion of the central processing unit executes all of the arithmetic and logical operations which the computer is instructed to perform.

assembly-level language. A programming language which substitutes one symbolic instruction for each machine-level language instruction. A program which translates the assembly-level instructions into machine-level is called an assembler.

*Information in this glossary has been drawn from various sources, including: American National Standards Institute, *American National Standard Vocabulary for Information Processing* (New York: American National Standards Institute, 1970); Susan Artandi, *An Introduction to Computers in Information Science* (Metuchen, N.J.: Scarecrow Press, 1972); Joseph Becker, *The First Book of Information Science* (Oak Ridge, Tenn.: U.S. Atomic Energy Commission, Office of Information Services, 1973); William Davis and Allison McCormack, *The Information Age* (Reading, Mass.: Addison-Wesley Publishing Co., 1979); Richard Dorf, *Computers and Man* (San Francisco: Boyd & Fraser Publishing Co., 1977); Mike Hyman and Eleanor Wallis, *Mini-Computers and Bibliographic Information Retrieval* (London: British Library, 1976); and Chris Mader, *Information Systems: Technology, Economics Applications, Management* (Chicago: Science Research Association, 1979).

authority file. A standard list of terms acceptable for a given function.

automatic data processing (ADP). Data processing largely performed by automatic means.

automatic indexing. An indexing process in which index terms are derived by a computer directly from the natural language text of a document. This method requires that the text of a document be available in machine-readable form.

automation. The investigation, design, development, and application of methods and equipment for making processing automatic.

batch processing. A type of computer processing in which all computer operations for a given function are programmed in advance so that the computer controls everything from the beginning to the end of the job. Normally, in batch processing, computing jobs are submitted to an operator to be processed sequentially, and, when each job is finished, the results are returned to the user.

binary code. A code that uses only two distinct characters, usually 0 and 1.

binary number system. A counting system in which the base or radix is two; accordingly, this sytem has only two symbols.

bit. A contraction of the term binary digit, a bit is the smallest unit used to represent information in a binary number system.

bits per inch (bpi). The recording density of data storage on magnetic tape is commonly measured in bits per inch.

Boolean Logic. A method of inquiry that restricts responses to yes or no and includes the logical operators, "and," "or," "not," "except," "if," and "then," which may be combined in a variety of ways.

bpi. See bits per inch.

bug. An error or malfunction.

byte. A sequence of adjacent binary digits (bits) operated upon as a unit. In most cases a byte is eight digits in length.

cathode ray tube (CRT). A device that displays data in visual form by means of controlled electron beams.

central processing unit (CPU). That portion of the hardware of a computer system which controls the interpretation and execution of instructions. The CPU includes the arithmetic unit, which performs arithmetic and logical operations, and the control unit, which directs the order of operation of the other hardware units and supervises the overall operation of the computer.

character. A letter, digit, or other symbol that is used in the organization, control, or representation of data.

COBOL (COmmon Business Oriented Language). A common programming language developed for business data processing.

COM. See computer output microfilm.

computer. A data processing device that can perform substantial computation, including numerous arithmetic or logic operations, without intervention by a human operator during the process. A computer is capable of solving problems by accepting data, performing specific operations on the data, and supplying the results of these operations.

computer output microfilm (COM). Information on microfilm which has been automatically transferred from a machine-readable format to a microform.

computer science. The study of computers and the phenomena resulting from their use.

control unit. In a digital computer, that portion of the central processing unit which directs the order of operation of other hardware units and supervises the overall operation of the computer. The control unit effects the retrieval of instructions in proper sequence, the interpretation of each instruction, and the application of the proper signals to the arithmetic unit.

controlled vocabulary. A type of indexing in which index terms are drawn from a predetermined standard listing of words and phrases called an authority file.

CPU. See central processing unit.

CRT. See cathode ray tube.

cylinder. In a disk pack all of the tracks, stacked on top of each other, that can be accessed without moving the access arm. Conceptually, these tracks form a vertical cylinder passing through the disk pack.

data. A representation of facts, concepts, or instructions in a formalized manner suitable for communication, interpretation, or processing by humans or by automatic means.

data base. Large, accumulated files of data for subsequent access by users. These files are usually in machine-readable form and are accessed via a computer.

data field. See field.

data or information processing. The execution of a systematic sequence of operations performed upon data. In practice, the term "data processing" is often used to refer to all computer-related activities.

data tag. see field-tag.

debug. The detection, location, and removal of errors from software or malfunctions from a computer.

descriptor. A word or phrase used as an indexing term.

digital computer. A computer that accepts and processes data represented by discrete symbols, such as letters of the alphabet, numbers, or algebraic and business symbols.

direct access. Pertaining to the process of obtaining data from, or placing data into, any location within a storage device in a constant amount of time.

diskette. See floppy disk.

disk pack. A stack of magnetic disks which are fixed onto a common spindle.

documentation. Information that is required to develop, operate, and maintain machine-readable files and data processing systems. Program documentation consists of program listings, flowcharts, narrative descriptions, data formats, and any other information that may assist in the use and maintenance of the programs.

EDP. See electronic data processing.

electronic data processing (EDP). Data processing largely performed by devices operated by means of electrical and electronic phenomena.

electronic digital computer. An information processing machine which can perform substantial computation, including numerous arithmetic or logic operations, without intervention by a human operator during the process.

electronic photocomposition. The combining of information stored on magnetic tape with high-speed photocomposition machines that automatically set type for printing.

field. In a record, a specified area with a clearly defined function which is used to enter a specific category of data. In some data processing systems each field is assigned a fixed number of positions or characters (fixed-length fields), in other systems the length of the fields may vary within defined limits (variable-length fields.)

field-tag. An alpha/numeric code used to identify a data field.

file. A collection of related records treated as a unit. A file usually contains records of similar type used for a common purpose.

fixed-length field. See field.

floppy disk. A small, flexible, magnetic disk with relatively limited storage capacity. Floppy disks (diskettes) usually consist of a single recording surface and are often used on minicomputers, microcomputers, or intelligent terminals.

flowchart. A graphic representation for the definition, analysis, or solution of a problem, in which symbols are used to represent operations, data flow, equipment, etc.

FORTRAN (FORmula TRANslator). A common programming language primarily used to express computer programs by arithmetic formulas.

hard copy. A printed copy of computer output in visually readable form.

hardware. Physical equipment used for processing data, as opposed to computer programs or methods of use. Hardware consists of the central processing unit, main storage units, input and output devices, and related components for storage, communication, and display of data.

hardwired. The connection of a computer terminal directly to a central processing unit rather than through telephone lines.

high-level language. A programming language in which each instruction or statement corresponds to several instructions in the corresponding machine-level langugage program, greatly reducing the number of instructions needed to be written by the programmer. A program which translates high-level instructions into machine-level is called a compiler.

information. The meaning that humans assign to data.

information retrieval. The technique and process of accumulating, organizing, storing, and searching large quantities of data, extracting and reproducing or displaying the required information contained within the data.

information science. The study of how humans create, use and communicate information.

input/output (I/O). A general term applied to the equipment used to communicate with a computer, the data involved in such communication, and the media carrying the data.

intelligent (or smart) terminal. A cross between a minicomputer or microcomputer and an I/O terminal, intelligent terminals have some memory and processing circuitry built in and may also have cassette tape storage or floppy-disk drives. Thus, some processing and storage may be done at the terminal site.

interactive computing. A type of computer processing that allows a user to interact directly with the computer. In a conversational manner, the computer acknowledges and acts upon requests entered by the user at a terminal.

I/O. See input/output.

key-to-disk. Hardware designed to transfer data entered at a keyboard to magnetic disk; also, the process of transferring data from a keyboard to a magnetic disk.

key-to-tape. Hardware designed to transfer data entered at a keyboard to magnetic tape; also, the process of transferring data from a keyboard to a magnetic tape.

keyword in context (KWIC). An indexing method based on the idea that words extracted from document titles, abstracts, and texts can be used effectively as indexing terms. In a KWIC index the keywords are printed in alphabetical order, together with the words surrounding the keyword.

keyword out of context (KWOC). An indexing method based on the idea that words extracted from document titles, abstracts, and texts can be used effectively as indexing terms. In a KWOC index extracted keywords are printed separately at the lefthand margin, and the keyword and the words surrounding it are printed to the right.

KWIC. See keyword in context.

KWOC. See keyword out of context.

language processing. The use of computers to manipulate words and ideas for functional purposes.

line printer. A computer-driven device that prints all the characters of a line as a unit. Various line printers operate at speeds ranging from 100 lines per minute (lpm) up to 3,000 lpm, however, 1,000 to 1,500 lpm is typical.

machine-level language. A language which may be directly understood by a computer, but in which program writing is difficult and tedious. Programs written in languages more easily used by humans can be automatically translated into machine-level language.

machine-readable. Information in a form, such as holes punched in cards or electronic signals encoded on a magnetic tape or disk, that can be processed directly by a computer.

magnetic disk. A flat, circular platter with a magnetic surface on which data can be stored by selective magnetization of portions of the flat surface. A disk can hold many files of data, stored in circular tracks, each with a unique location.

magnetic ink character recognition (MICR). A data entry method widely used by the banking industry. Each character to be entered is imprinted with magnetic ink; an optical scanning device can then electrically sense and identify each character.

magnetic tape. A tape with a magnetizable ferrous oxide coating on which data can be stored by selective polarizations of portions of the surface.

main memory. The basic data storage component of a computer. Main memory accepts data from input units, exchanges data and instructions with the central processing unit, and furnishes information to output units; all data to be processed must pass through this unit.

MC/ST. Magnetic Card/Selectric Typewriter.

MICR. See magnetic ink character recognition.

microcomputer. A very small computer, often used for a special purpose or single function. Its low cost and popularity with computer hobbyists is producing rapid growth in its sale and useful applications.

minicomputer. A general term used to describe small, digital computers. Sometimes these small computers function as a component of a larger system; other minicomputers function independently and perform many of the operations characteristic of larger computers.

natural language. A type of indexing in which index terms are drawn from a nonrestricted vocabulary and not limited exclusively to words and phrases which appear in the indexed material.

OCR. See optical character recognition.

off-line. A term applied to devices and data that are not directly controlled by the central processing unit.

on-line. A term applied to devices and data directly controlled by the central processing unit. On-line also refers to a user's ability to interact directly with a computer.

on-line data entry. A process in which an operator uses a terminal to key input data directly to the computer. On-line data entry makes substantial logic and editing capabilities immediately available to the data entry operator.

operating system. System software which controls the execution of computer programs and which may provide scheduling, debugging, input/output control, accounting, compilation, storage assignment, data management, and related services.

optical character recognition (OCR). A data entry method in which an optical scanning device can be used to read almost any type of printed material and some hand-printed material and automatically convert the data to a machine-readable form.

optical scanning. The automatic conversion of data into a machine-readable form by visual pattern detection techniques.

peripheral equipment. Any unit of computer hardware, distinct from the central processing unit and the main storage unit, which may provide a data processing system with outside communication.

postcoordinate indexing. A method of indexing which allows free manipulation of indexing terms at the time of searching. Thus, the user is able to develop logical term combinations appropriate to his or her query.

precoordinate indexing. A method of indexing in which term relationship coordination is done at the time of indexing. Documents are searched under the same terms which the indexer originally assigned to them, without further manipulation of terms at the time of searching.

printout. The most common form of computer output on which computer-processed information is printed by a line printer.

program. A detailed and explicit set of instructions presented in a form that can be interpreted by a computer.

programmer. An individual primarily involved in the designing, writing, and testing of computer programs.

programming. The process of planning the functional steps necessary for a computer to accomplish a specific function, and then writing the instructions for the performance of this function in a language or notation that can be interpreted by a computer.

programming or source language. A special language or notation in which computer programs are written.

004198 (9)
(In error)

punched card. A stiff paper card punched with a pattern of holes to represent data.

punched paper tape. A narrow strip of paper on which data can be recorded as a pattern of punched holes.

read/write head. A device which writes data to or reads data from a magnetic recording medium.

record. A collection of related items of data (see field) treated as a unit. A record consists of all data fields related to some common entity. In some systems, a record is assigned a fixed number of characters (fixed-length record); in other systems the length of each record is allowed to vary within the defined limits (variable-length record).

register. A device which stores, temporarily, small amounts of data in the central processing unit. This device accepts, stores, and releases electrical pulses under the direction of the control unit.

seek arm. See access arm.

sequential access. A method of accessing computer records one after another in physical sequence. Access time for requested data is dependent on its physical location on the storage device.

smart terminal. See intelligent terminal.

software. A set of programs, procedures, rules, and associated documentation concerned with the operation of a data processing system. Software is neither the physical portion of an information system nor the data to be manipulated; software refers only to the sets of instructions that direct the functioning of computer hardware.

stoplist. A group of minor words, such as prepositions, conjunctions, and articles, which a computer is instructed to disregard in its selection of indexing terms. Words included in stoplists vary, depending on which words are considered to lack meaning for indexing in a particular application.

storage. A device into which data can be entered, held, and from which it can be obtained at a later time.

system. An assembly of methods, procedures, techniques, machinery, or personnel united by regulated interaction to form a whole or to accomplish a set of specific functions.

system software. Programs that belong to the entire system rather than to any single user and that usually perform a support function.

tag. See field-tag.

terminal. A piece of hardware designed for the purpose of entering data or obtaining data from a computer. A keyboard terminal has a typewriter-like keyboard and is often equipped with a cathode ray tube (CRT) for visual display of data being sent to or returned from a computer.

thesaurus. A structured controlled vocabulary which has links from each term to its various associated terms. The five common types of associated terms are: (1) broader terms (less specific), (2) narrower terms (more specific), (3) related terms (at a similar level of specificity with a common broader term), (4) homonymous terms (same terms used to describe different subjects), and (5) synonymous terms (different terms used to describe a single subject).

time-sharing. The use of a central computer by numerous users in different locations at the same time. At a terminal each user can do separate tasks on the same computer, yet all users seem to get service simultaneously.

tracks. See magnetic disk.

turnaround time. The elapsed time between the submission of a job to be run on a computer and the return of the results.

variable-length field. See field.

word processing. A concept that views words as products and an office as a facility for producing words. Word processing equipment has been designed to help transcribe, replay, power type, edit, reproduce, store, and transmit words.

Acknowledgments

In writing this manual, I have drawn on a variety of sources of advice and information. I visited several archival programs to examine their use of automation and to discuss the implications of adopting automated techniques. Without exception I received courteous and valuable assistance from the staff of these institutions and would like to express my gratitude to John Knowlton and Steven Hensen of the Library of Congress Manuscript Division; Diane Vogt of the Corning Glass Works Archives; Adele Newberger of the Baltimore Region Institutional Studies Center; Lee McDonald, Hugo Stibbe, Vivian Cartmell, and Grace Hyam of the Public Archives of Canada; David Bearman of the Survey of Sources for the History of Biochemistry and Molecular Biology; Stephanie Sykes of the University of Western Ontario; Richard Lytle and Alan Bain of the Smithsonian Institution Archives; Ruth Helmuth, Laura Gorretta, Virginia Krumholtz, and Esther Greenberg of Case Western Reserve University; Maynard Brichford and William Maher of the University of Illinois at Urbana-Champaign; and Max Evans of the State Historical Society of Wisconsin. Time to carry out these visits was provided by a research leave from Cornell University Libraries, and I want to thank Herbert Finch, Assistant University Librarian for Special Collections, for his consistent support of my efforts.

Those who read and commented on the manuscript include Richard Lytle, Max Evans, Virginia Purdy, and Meyer Fishbein. I am especially indebted to David Bearman and Elaine Engst, who provided me with many useful suggestions on how the work might be improved. Jane Gustafson efficiently typed and retyped the original manuscript, and Julia Crepeau typed further revisions. Final preparation of the manuscript was ably carried out by Joyce Gianatasio and Deborah Risteen. I also gratefully acknowledge the cooperation and comradeship of the staff of the Cornell Department of Manuscripts and University Archives, whose support has been invaluable. Finally, I thank the members of my family, Ann, Greg, Tim, Angela, and Caryn, whose direct and indirect contributions have been considerable.

H. Thomas Hickerson
Cornell University

H. Thomas Hickerson is Chairman of the Department of Manuscripts and University Archives at Cornell University. He was formerly Head of the Oklahoma State Archives and Records Division.